MODERN WORLD NATIONS

AFGHANISTAN	ISRAEL
ARGENTINA	ITALY
AUSTRALIA	JAMAICA
AUSTRIA	JAPAN
BAHRAIN	KAZAKHSTAN
BANGLADESH	KENYA
BERMUDA	KUWAIT
BOLIVIA	MEXICO
BOSNIA AND HERZEGOVINA	THE NETHERLANDS
BRAZIL	NEW ZEALAND
CANADA	NIGERIA
CHILE	NORTH KOREA
CHINA	NORWAY
COSTA RICA	PAKISTAN
CROATIA	PERU
CUBA	THE PHILIPPINES
DEMOCRATIC REPUBLIC OF THE CONGO	PORTUGAL
	PUERTO RICO
EGYPT	RUSSIA
ENGLAND	SAUDI ARABIA
ETHIOPIA	SCOTLAND
FRANCE	SENEGAL
REPUBLIC OF GEORGIA	SOUTH AFRICA
GERMANY	SOUTH KOREA
GHANA	SPAIN
GREECE	SWEDEN
GUATEMALA	TAIWAN
ICELAND	THAILAND
INDIA	TURKEY
INDONESIA	UKRAINE
IRAN	UZBEKISTAN
IRAQ	VENEZUELA
IRELAND	VIETNAM

Thailand

Douglas A. Phillips

Series Editor
Charles F. Gritzner
South Dakota State University

An imprint of Infobase Publishing

Frontispiece: Flag of Thailand

Cover: Buddhist temple in Bangkok, Thailand.

Thailand

Copyright © 2007 by Infobase Publishing

Chelsea House
An imprint of Infobase Publishing
132 West 31st Street
New York NY 10001

ISBN-10: 0-7910-9250-X
ISBN-13: 978-0-7910-9250-7

Library of Congress Cataloging-in-Publication Data

Phillips, Douglas A.
  Thailand / Douglas A. Phillips.
    p. cm. — (Modern world nations)
  Includes bibliographical references and index.
  ISBN 0-7910-9250-X (hardcover)
  1. Thailand—Juvenile literature. I. Title. II. Series.

  DS563.5.P455 2007
  959.3—dc22   2006032009

Chelsea House books are available at special discounts when purchased in bulk quantities for businesses, associations, institutions, or sales promotions. Please call our Special Sales Department in New York at (212) 967-8800 or (800) 322-8755.

You can find Chelsea House on the World Wide Web at http://www.chelseahouse.com

Series and Cover design by Takeshi Takahashi

Printed in the United States of America

Bang Hermitage 10 9 8 7 6 5 4 3 2 1

This book is printed on acid-free paper.

All links, Web addresses, and Internet search terms were checked and verified to be correct at the time of publication. Because of the dynamic nature of the Web, some addresses and links may have changed since publication and may no longer be valid.

Table of Contents

1   Introducing Thailand   8

2   Physical Landscapes   14

3   Thailand Through Time   24

4   People and Culture   39

5   Government and Politics   50

6   Thailand's Economy   65

7   Major Urban Areas in Thailand   77

8   Thailand Looks Ahead   86

    Facts at a Glance   92
    History at a Glance   95
    Bibliography   98
    Further Reading   99
    Index   101

This book is dedicated to our three incredible children, Christopher Phillips, Angela Phillips Burnett, and Daniel Phillips. All three have been and continue to be teachers to my wife, Marlene, and me. From tiny little wonders to talented loving adults, they have taught us all along the way and reminded us daily of the power of a smile and a laugh. Even though each is very unique and gifted, their shared strength is their character, a trait that will serve them and others forever. My love and respect for these incredible individuals is unbounded.

Thailand

Introducing Thailand

*S*awaddee! Welcome to Thailand! *Sawaddee* is an all-purpose greeting that can mean good morning, good afternoon, good evening, or good night. By putting your palms gently together under your chin with your head tilted slightly forward, you have greeted your hosts with the *wai* (form of greeting) that is used in Thailand. If you want to be even more appropriate, use the wai and say "Sawaddee krup" (if you are a man) or "Sawaddee ka" (if you are a woman). With this greeting, you have not only shown respect to your host, but you also have started your amazing adventure into the exploration of Thailand.

Thailand was formerly known as the Kingdom of Siam until the country's name was changed to Thailand in 1939. This fascinating country is an ancient place with hospitable people and a complex culture that dates back more than 800 years. The list of cultural what to do's and what not to do's is extensive, but the Thai are very accepting of foreigners who try to participate. For example, one should not touch the head of a Thai person. Most Thais are Buddhists, and the head, being the highest part of the body, is considered sacred. At the other end, the feet—being the body's lowest point—are viewed as being dirty. Thus, a person should never expose the bottom of his or her feet or shoes to others; neither should feet be used to point at someone. These customs also apply to statues of Buddha and even photos of the king. Another cultural practice is to not wai a child, because it is considered bad luck. These are just a few of the interesting cultural practices of the Thai people.

Exploring Thailand is truly a unique experience. For example, in the north, there are a number of hill tribes, such as those of the Karen people, who live in both Thailand and Myanmar (formerly Burma). Each tribe possesses its own culture and cultural practices, including some that are quite unique. The Karen Padaung tribe, near the city of Chiang Mai, is quite small, but is well known because of their long-neck women. Brass rings are added each year to lengthen the neck of women, which is regarded as being a sign of beauty. A long-neck woman in Plam Piang Din Village wears an incredible 37 brass rings! In another Karen tribe, women wear carved elephant tusks in their ears as a sign of beauty. These women are often called Long-ears.

Not all Thai people are like the Karen tribes. Today, most Thais live in cities or agricultural areas in this tropical country. Bangkok is the capital and the largest urban center. It is an amazing city with world-class transportation, banking, industry, and services. At the same time, it is a city choked with traffic and pollution. Modern vehicles crawl along the roads fighting for space with three-wheeled taxis called *tuk-tuks*. These vehicles can provide a visitor with an unforgettable yet sometimes frightening experience.

Thailand is a treasure trove of culture, history, and amazing physical geography. This Southeast Asian country stretches from the mountains of the north to the gorgeous white beach

In Thailand, the Karen Padaung people live in three villages near the border with Myanmar. The tribe is known for its distinctive "long-neck" women who wear decorative brass coils around their necks.

sands in the south. It extends from the vast Khorat Plateau region and the Mekong River in the northeast to the mountainous and often contested border region with Myanmar to the west. Four countries border Thailand: Myanmar to the west and northwest, Laos to the northeast, Cambodia to the east, and Malaysia to the south. The Andaman Sea and the Gulf of Thailand are respectively on the west and east of peninsular Thailand.

Thailand has a total area of 198,115 square miles (513,115 square kilometers). This is an area about twice the size of the state of Wyoming. The coastline totals about 2,000 miles (3,219 kilometers), while the land boundaries with neighboring countries totals 3,022 miles (4,863 kilometers). The population of Thailand was estimated in July of 2006 to be about 65 million, or nearly 326 people per square mile (126 per square kilometer).

Thailand's history has proven to be like a walk on a tightrope. It is the only Southeast Asian country that was not colonized by Europeans. To avoid colonial occupation, the country's kings often danced a fine line between the European powers and often played them off against each other. This high-wire tradition of maintaining political independence was evident during both of the twentieth century's World Wars. In World War I, Siam joined the Allies in 1917. In World War II, Thailand first became an ally of Japan and intended to declare war on the United States and the United Kingdom. However, the Thai ambassador to the United States refused to deliver the declaration, so the United States never reciprocated by declaring war on Thailand. This strange turn of events was one of the most interesting diplomatic feats accomplished by a country during the twentieth century.

Thai politics in the twentieth century have been typified by revolving civilian and military governments. The government has recently been a constitutional monarchy ruling under a constitution that was adopted in 1997. However, a military coup in 2006 suspended that constitution. The primary source for stability during Thailand's turbulent times has been the king. At times, he has taken the side of either the military or the civilian government. The king's power is tremendous, although not necessarily drawn from the constitution. Thais have a level

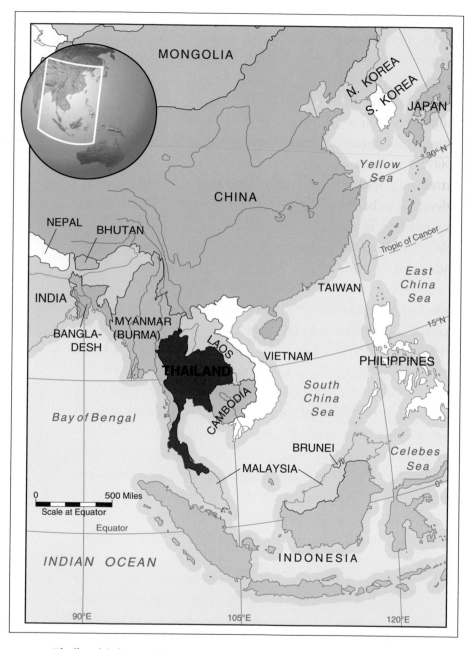

Thailand is located in Southeast Asia and shares borders with four
countries: Laos and Cambodia to the east, Myanmar to the west, and
Malaysia to the south. The country is about twice the size of Wyoming
and is home to more than 64 million people.

of respect and reverence for their king that is virtually un-matched in the world today. Some view him almost as a god. Fortunately, most of the kings have been very benevolent to the people and have acted in their best interests. The present monarch, King Bhumibol Adulyadej, is the longest-reigning monarch in the world today. He was born in 1927 and he assumed the throne in 1946. A major celebration took place in 2006 to celebrate his sixtieth anniversary as king. He remains extremely popular with the people of Thailand, and they consider him to be the reason that their democratic government was installed in 1992. In this book, readers will find that the role of the king can never be underestimated in Thai politics and society.

Thus our adventure begins! The following chapters will unfold the incredible story of Thailand and its people. From tightrope walks to unique cultures and from political and economic prosperity to devastating disaster, the story will help the reader to understand this complex and attractive place. Millions of tourists flock to Thailand every year to see the beauty and experience the Thai people and culture. Have a wonderful journey as you read through these pages.

2

Physical Landscapes

T hailand is blessed with a beautiful natural environment. The country possesses features that run from misty mountain areas overlooking lush green rice paddies to vast lands covered by tropical rain forests. Sites like Phang Nga Bay and extensive coral reefs provide a range of visual treats that entice millions to the country. There are beautiful beaches, mountains, and rain forests. Wild animals such as elephants, tapirs, sloths, bears, and even tigers roam the countryside. The cities of Bangkok, Chiang Mai, and Phuket are often the sights that visitors hear about. But the country also offers many other hidden natural treasures to examine.

The physical environment serves much like a stage for human activities. In this chapter, we will examine Thailand's land features, weather and climate, and natural hazards. The country's natural landscapes provide a strikingly attractive stage that humans have impacted in both positive and negative ways.

LAND FEATURES AND NATURAL REGIONS

Thailand can be divided into four different regions based on its land features: the northern region, the Khorat Plateau, the central region, and the southern region. Each region has distinct physical traits that define it and make it different from other areas of the country. And in each, humans have utilized the land and its resources in a variety of different ways.

The Northern Region

The northern region features rugged uplands, with Doi Inthanon being the highest mountain at 8,451 feet (2,576 meters). This region borders eastern Myanmar and western Laos, and encompasses part of the famous (or infamous) Golden Triangle, an area known as an illegal opium-growing region. This region was home to Thailand's earliest civilization and is home today to many of Thailand's colorful tribal people like the Karen.

Many rivers are located in the northern region, including the Ping, Wang, Yom, and Nan, which converge to form the Chao Phraya at Nakhon Sawan. The mountains and rivers provide many breathtaking views that serve to attract tourists. Wildlife sanctuaries and numerous national parks provide protection for lands and animals that have been threatened by deforestation and hunting. Doi Inthanon National Park is only one of the parks in the region. This park is a visual masterpiece marked by waterfalls, expansive views, and vegetation that includes wild orchids and other beautiful flora.

Relative to the rest of the country, the north has a cooler climate. Economic activities include the harvesting of teak, an extremely valuable hardwood. Crops such as lychee (or litchi, a tropical fruit), mandarin oranges, mango, melons, and strawberries are grown, along with ever-present rice crops. On the negative side, the region also produces crops that are illegal in much of the world. Poppy fields, the source of opium, have long dotted the region's agricultural landscape. More recently,

Thailand is made up of four distinct geographic regions: the mountainous
north; the Khorat Plateau in the northeast; the Chao Phraya River Valley
in the central part of the country; and the tropical Malay Peninsula and
Kra Isthmus in the south.

poppies have been used to produce heroin. The region is believed to be the second-largest producer of opium today, trailing only Afghanistan.

The Khorat Plateau

Northeastern Thailand is defined by the Khorat Plateau, which borders the mighty Mekong River, which, in turn, serves as the eastern border with Laos. The massive, flat, and relatively barren Khorat Plateau covers about 60,000 square miles (155,000 square kilometers), or one-third of the country. It is drained by two major rivers, the Mun and Chi, which both empty into the Mekong. Because of its relatively low elevation, 300 to 650 feet (90 to 200 meters) above sea level, it offers little relief from the tropical temperatures. The plateau region is separated from central Thailand by the Phetchabun Mountains on the west and from Cambodia on the south by the Phnom Dangrek Range.

The Khorat Plateau also features flora and fauna that is suitable to the region. For example, except near the Mekong River, the region's forests are composed of trees adapted to drier conditions. Hard ground makes it difficult for the soil to soak up the monsoon rains. In fact, water tends to pool at the surface, causing frequent floods during the rainy season, which runs from April to October. Cotton, rice, peanuts, corn, and hemp are grown by people in the region. Cattle, horses, and pigs also are raised.

The Central Region

The central region of the country is wrapped around the Chao Phraya River Valley, which runs southward into the Gulf of Thailand. The Chao Phraya has created a rich alluvial (stream-deposited soil or sand) plain that is bordered by the Phetchabun Mountains in the east and the Dawna and Bilauktaung ranges that separate Thailand from Myanmar in the west. The alluvial plain is relatively flat and extremely fertile. Because of

Bangkok is Thailand's capital and largest city, with more than 6 million residents. The city is a popular tourist destination and is also the country's chief port.

the flat terrain and richness of the soil, about 40 percent of Thailand's population lives here, on about 30 percent of the country's land.

Within the central region are the cities of Bangkok and Ayutthaya. The region also has served as host for most of the great civilizations in Thailand's past. This is also the country's major agricultural area, with the rich soil serving as a welcome host for the vitally important crop of rice. Because of the river-enriched soils, the Chao Phraya is called the Menom, or "mother of waters," by the Thai people. Forests and agriculture dominate land use, with both occupying about half of the region.

The Southern Region

Southern Thailand stretches along the Malay Peninsula and the slender Kra Isthmus, which is bordered by the Gulf of Thailand on the east and the Bay of Bengal and Strait of Malacca on the west. The Thai-Malaysia border is on the south, and Myanmar borders the region on the west. This region represents only about one-seventh of the country's land area, but it has its own distinctive personality. Mountain chains dot the region, which also includes many Thai islands. The Kra Isthmus has often been discussed as a possible location for a canal to connect the waters on the east and west of Thailand. Such an endeavor would make long trade journeys around the Malay Peninsula much shorter and less expensive. In addition, a canal would relieve sea traffic in the congested Strait of Malacca, which forms the main ship passageway between the Indian Ocean and the Pacific Ocean.

The southern region is covered with rain forests and is rich in minerals. This section of Thailand receives the most rainfall. It is also the region that attracts many tourists, who are drawn by its pristine sandy beaches and coral reefs, distinctive islands, and picturesque fishing villages.

WEATHER AND CLIMATE

Thailand has two distinct climate regions. In the south, it is humid tropical, and in the north, it is tropical savanna. The climate of the Kra Isthmus is always hot and humid, and intermittent rains fall throughout the year. The north is usually more comfortable, with temperatures 6° to 9°F (3° to 5°C) lower than those in the south. The country as a whole is tropical, humid, and rainy. These conditions must be taken into consideration by tourists if they are to be comfortable during their trip. Temperatures are nearly always quite high, and humidity rarely drops below 70 percent anywhere in the country.

Three seasons are evident in the northern, plateau, and central regions. The warmest time of the year is from March to May. Temperatures may reach into the upper 90s°F (mid-30s °C) with high humidity that makes conditions seem even hotter. The monsoon season, with its drenching rains, begins in mid-May and continues though September. During this time of the year, afternoon high temperatures drop into the mid-80s°F (29–30°C). Because it is the wet season, however, the humidity averages 90 to 100 percent, which makes summer an uncomfortable time of the year. Rain showers are frequent, and often torrential, but usually brief. Flooding sometimes occurs during the monsoon season. Fortunately, Thailand does not suffer from frequent and devastating floods that occur in nearby countries such as Bangladesh and India. The third season, running from November through February, is cooler. This more comfortable time of year results from a reverse wind flow, called a dry monsoon, with northeast winds that bring cooler and drier conditions. Temperatures during this time of the year are usually from the upper 70s to low 80s°F (25–28°C).

Southern Thailand has only two seasons, so there is less variance in temperature over the course of the year. The south is affected by both the wet and dry monsoons, but to a much lesser degree than in the other three regions. The dry monsoon is much shorter than in the north, because the nearby waters keep the humidity high and rainfall more frequent.

ENVIRONMENTAL HAZARDS

Unfortunately, Thailand does have some natural elements that on occasion threaten land, property, and human life. For example, on December 26, 2004, a devastating tsunami struck Khao Lak, Phuket, and other coastline areas on the Andaman Sea. A tsunami is an ocean wave generated by a submarine earthquake or volcanic movement. The December 2004 tsunami was triggered by a magnitude 9.0 earthquake near Indonesia. It crossed the Andaman Sea in just over two hours, swept ashore, and

The resort of Khao Lak was devastated by the massive tsunami that struck Thailand in December 2004. At least 4,000 residents and vacationers were killed by the tidal wave and the tourist industry has yet to recover. Pictured here is an elephant helping to clear debris near Bang Nieng Beach in Khao Lak, one week after the tsunami.

battered Khao Lak, leaving the city in tattered, muddy, drenched ruins. In mere minutes, thousands of people died, and hotels, beach sands, and vegetation were stripped from the coastline.

Other natural hazards that can affect Thailand are occasional floods, droughts, earthquakes, cyclones (hurricanes), and occasional landslides. Droughts and earthquakes have caused almost no loss of life in recent decades, but the country has a surprising vulnerability to droughts. Floods and cyclones, however, have more impact. During the twentieth century, more than 2,000 people died in floods and nearly 1,500 died as a result of cyclones during the same time period.

With these threats, Thailand has developed early warning systems such as the Bangkok Tropical Cyclone Warning Center.

Others are being developed, including an early tsunami warning system that would help avoid a repeat of the disastrous 2004 tsunami. The country is also analyzing the causes of droughts and their consequences. Drought-related problems include not only inconsistent rainfall distribution, but also shallow water reservoirs, low water holding capacity of soil, and the erosion of sediment.

HUMAN IMPACT ON THE ENVIRONMENT

People can have various impacts on their environment, some helpful and others very damaging. Thailand is no different in this respect, and humans have left their imprint on the environment in a number of ways. The splendor of the Golden Temple in Bangkok is one example of a pleasing impact that people can have on the landscape. So is the haunting beauty of the ancient capital of Ayutthaya, which is encircled by three rivers. Unfortunately, humans often inflict considerable damage on the environment in which they live.

Air and water pollution are major environmental issues facing Thailand today, with Bangkok and other cities literally choked by the poor air quality and filthy water. The World Bank estimates that these two types of pollution lower the country's gross domestic product (GDP) by 1.6 percent to 2.6 percent each year. In 1992, the United Nations Environment Programme (UNEP) designated Bangkok as one of the worst cities in the world in terms of air pollution. The United States-Asia Environmental Partnership (US-AEP) estimates that in Thailand alone, 2,300 people die each year because of air pollution. Cars and other vehicles, power plants, factories, forest fires, agricultural burning, and open cooking on a fire all contribute to the massive problem of air pollution in Thailand. Thai laws passed in the 1990s have been responsible for creating programs to improve the air quality but much still needs to be done.

Water pollution in Thailand is caused mainly by agricultural runoff, industrial waste, human sewage and other waste, and aquaculture (the artificial raising of seafood such as shrimp) along the coast. The US-AEP estimates that half of the lakes and rivers in Thailand have poor water quality. Water pollution has a negative impact, because it affects a basic human need for clean drinking water. Recent efforts designed to improve the quality of Thailand's water supply have met with some success. But the country still has a long way to go before its waters will be safe.

Soil erosion and deforestation are also negative manifestations of human impact on the environment. About 80 percent of Thailand was once forested. The loss of rain forests proceeded at an alarming rate during the twentieth century. By 1960, only 50 percent of the land was still forested. During the 13-year span from 1976 to 1989, deforestation accelerated, with another 28 percent of the forest cover being lost. Between 1990 and 2005, another 9.1 percent was harvested. Today, the country is less than 20 percent forested. Much of the clearing has been done to make land suitable for crop production. Deforestation has also increased soil erosion and decreased biodiversity. Thailand once had the world's second-richest rain forests in terms of biodiversity. Decades of development, however, have encroached upon the country's plant and animal life and placed it in severe jeopardy. However, as a party to the Convention on Biological Diversity, Thailand is now conducting a variety of efforts to protect its rich biodiversity.

Thailand's natural environment has provided a rich atmosphere for the country to develop. The country's four tropical regions all have unique qualities, but all are being threatened today by human impacts. Rapid population growth and expanding patterns of human settlement further encroach upon the country's natural environment. Human ingenuity is challenged by the necessity of balancing human needs with those of nature's ecosystems. Finding environmentally friendly solutions that will allow the country to continue its economic development along with population growth will be of extreme importance in the twenty-first century.

3

Thailand Through Time

The Kingdom of Siam conjures up images of times long ago in the exotic Far East. Movies such as *The King and I* (1956), featuring Yul Brynner and Deborah Kerr, and the remake, entitled *Anna and the King* (1999), with Jodie Foster and Yun-Fat Chow, have popularized this exotic perception of Thailand. People visiting Thailand also report very favorable views of the former Kingdom of Siam and its rich Buddhist culture.

Thailand has a fascinating past that is unique from that of its neighbors. As noted in Chapter 1, it is the only country in the region never to have been colonized by outsiders. As a result, Thailand has independently developed its own relationships with countries within the region and throughout the Western world. The first independent Thai kingdom dates back in time nearly eight centuries, to 1238, and the country has remained independent since that time. As a Buddhist country, it has often followed the middle road. In fact, Buddha no doubt would have been pleased to witness the political course that the country has navigated through history.

THE FIRST PEOPLE

Not much is known about early Thai peoples. People are known to have been in Southeast Asia for nearly one-half million years. Others speculate that people lived in the Mekong River Valley and the Khorat Plateau up to 10,000 years ago. Rice-cultivating tribal cultures existed in the Ban Chieng area of northeastern Thailand more than 5,000 years ago. Thus, the people of Ban Chieng were one of the earliest civilizations in the world to raise rice. These people also used bronze extensively in making musical instruments and cooking utensils. Some scientists believe that the Ban Chieng civilization may predate the Middle Eastern Bronze Age, because there is evidence of very early work with metal. The people of Ban Chieng also used pottery and textiles that were artistically decorated. Linguists trace the early Thai languages back to China, because this is where the early Thai (often spelled Tai in earlier eras) probably migrated from.

By A.D. 650, the early Thai people had established a kingdom called Nanchao in Yunnan, China. This kingdom remained independent until about 1000, at which time China laid claim to the territory, making it a satellite state. Originally, Nanchao served as a protective "buffer state" between the Chinese Tang Dynasty and strong neighbors like Tibet. Slowly, however, Nanchao turned against China, and this caused the kingdom to eventually fall under the Chinese sphere of influence. In 1253, the Mongols, under Kublai Khan, conquered China, thereby adding Nanchao to their empire, which is called the Yuan Dynasty.

Nanchao was not only important to China, but also to the development of Thailand. It served to buffer the region from the overwhelmingly powerful influence of Chinese culture and politics. This allowed the Kingdom of Sukhothai to form in 1238. This was the year that Thai tribal chiefs threw out the

Khmer and established the new kingdom. Translated to English *Sukhothai* means the "dawn of happiness." As Kublai Khan swept into China and later Nanchao, many people fled from these areas into Sukhothai. This helped the region to unite further. Today, Thais view this unification and the founding of the kingdom as truly a dawn of happiness for the nation. Present-day Thailand traces its national identity back to the founding of the Kingdom of Sukhothai.

King Ramkhamhaeng Kamheng came to power in 1277. He initiated the use of the Cambodian (Khmer) alphabet that is still used in the country today. Kamheng was a famous warrior who ruled the kingdom for 40 years. With his power and military might, he extended the kingdom farther southward along the Malay Peninsula and into neighboring areas. Today, he is referred to as Rama the Great, because Thais view his leadership as having been of key importance to the country's development. However, his successors were less successful, and after Rama the Great's death in 1317, the kingdom declined rapidly until it fell to the Thai kingdom of Ayutthaya, described next. An enduring legacy of the Sukhothai Dynasty is the Thai form of Theravada Buddhism that remains strong in the country today. Theravada Buddhism will be examined more deeply in Chapter 4, which describes Thai culture.

THE RISE OF AYUTTHAYA

Ayutthaya was founded in 1350 by U Thong. He was of Chinese descent and married into a royal family. To escape a cholera epidemic that was threatening the population, he moved his people from China and established his capital in the city of Ayutthaya. Ayutthaya was an island city located at a point where the Chao Phraya, Pasak, and Lopburi rivers join in present-day central Thailand. In Ayutthaya, U Thong (who assumed a royal name, Ramathibodi I, when he ascended to the throne) worked to unify this new southern Thai kingdom. In 1360, he also established Theravada Buddhism as the official religion. Ramathibodi

Founded in 1350 by King U Thong, Ayutthaya is located in central Thailand and once served as the capital of the Kingdom of Siam. Now a UNESCO World Heritage Site, the ruins of Ayutthaya are made up of several monasteries and temples, including Wat Chai Watthanaram temple (pictured here), which was built in 1630.

ruled until the time of his death in 1369. Key among his accomplishments was the establishment of a legal code based upon Thai customs and Hindu legal texts.

Ayutthaya continued as a regional power until 1767. The Chinese favored Ayutthaya over Sukhothai, and anointed Ayutthaya as the Thai kingdom in the late fourteenth century. Attempts were made by subsequent kings to expand the empire, but these were met with mixed results. The most notable gains were in the area of present-day Cambodia. There, Ayutthayan forces took a Khmer stronghold at Lopburi and later, in 1431, took the historic city of Ankor, which had been the Khmer capital. In the fifteenth century, Ayutthaya also tried to take more of the Malay Peninsula in order to play a larger role in the lucrative trade on the Strait of Malacca. They were unsuccessful in these attempts at expansion, but the trade of Ayutthaya continued to flourish.

Trade made Ayutthaya rich. Portuguese missionaries and traders began to arrive in 1511. Along with their trade, the Portuguese brought their religion and aided Ayutthaya in its battles with the Kingdom of Chiang Mai in northern Thailand. They provided new technology to Ayutthaya, including cannons and muskets. These weapons were vastly superior to the weapons possessed by hostile neighbors like Burma. Ayutthaya also effectively used diplomacy to avoid becoming a colony of the Portuguese or other European countries as contact with the West increased.

EUROPE KNOCKS AT THE DOOR

In 1592, the Dutch agreed to a rice treaty with Ayutthaya. This made the Netherlands the second European presence in Thailand. Soon after, the British and the French also became interested in Siam (as the land came to be known in the West), and negotiations and diplomacy began in earnest. European colonies were being formed throughout Asia as the grip of the West tightened on many of Siam's neighbors. Would Thailand's relationship with the European nations result in colonization as it had with so many of its neighbors, or would it lead to a different relationship?

European inroads into Siam continued with trade under King Narai, who ruled from 1657 until 1688. Even though he was skeptical of the Europeans, he extended trade with the British and Dutch, who were also permitted to build factories. New relationships with Japan were developed, and Narai sent diplomatic envoys to France and the Netherlands. King Narai was a skillful diplomat who often played European powers against one another, because they already had a basic mistrust of each other's interests in the region. By playing the Europeans against each other, no power was able to gain predominant control over Thailand. However, in 1664, the Dutch tried by force to dominate in Thailand, and King Narai called upon the French to counterbalance the Dutch. This was successful until the French also fell out of favor with Buddhist leaders and wealthy and influential members of Thai society. Thus, a healthy lack of trust in and dislike for Europeans was quickly becoming the prevailing attitude of Thai leaders.

When King Narai's health began to fail in the late 1680s, General Phra Phetracha killed Narai's heir to the throne and seized power. After taking the throne, he expelled the remaining Europeans and initiated a 150-year period during which Thailand had little contact with the Western world. This era of self-imposed isolation helped to usher in the perception in the West of Thailand as being a little-known, exotic, and forbidden place. Phetracha ruled from 1688 to 1693.

In all, Ayutthaya served as capital of Thailand for 417 years, from 1350 until 1767. Thirty-three kings and five dynasties moved the Ayutthaya-led country forward toward the eighteenth century, until the Burmese invasions in the 1760s. During the Ayutthaya era, European influence had been all but removed, and the country was one of the few in all of Asia to retain its independence. The country also had frequent skirmishes with its neighbors, including Burma, Laos, and Cambodia during the Ayutthaya era. Nonetheless, trade continued to flourish as rice, dried fish, and forest products were exported.

Internally, Ayutthaya society became more hierarchical with three social classes. The king and other nobility constituted the top. At the bottom were slaves and commoners, and a class in the middle consisted of officials. Buddhist leaders and monks were classless, because they could come from any of the three classes.

Thus, Buddhist monks cut across all three social classes. The kings were not only kings but divine rulers, and treated accordingly. Tying political leadership to the perception of the king as being divine started in the Ayutthaya era. Separation of the two ideas still remains difficult for many Thais even today.

The end of the Ayutthaya era was horrific, as three Burmese armies moved into the city in 1767 from different directions. Attacks were savage, and thousands of people were killed. Burmese soldiers plundered the city's riches, burned it, and left a devastating scar in the memory of the Thai people. The Burmese even melted down gold statues of Buddha for the precious metal. Lingering Thai resentment toward Burma still exists today from the events associated with the Burmese invasions that ended Ayutthaya's reign. The Burmese invasions left Ayutthaya's kingdom fragmented into smaller provinces that usually were led by military leaders. However, the Thais were fortunate in that they were not occupied by the Burmese. As luck would have it, China had invaded Burma's lands, diverting their attention and resources. Meanwhile, a new Thai military leader named Phraya Taksin rose to prominence.

Taksin successfully broke out of Ayutthaya, through the Burmese encirclement, and regrouped his forces. Seven months later, he returned to push the weakened Burmese out of Ayutthaya. Taksin then proceeded to establish his capital in the city of Thonburi, across the river from Bangkok, and he was made king in December 1767. Under his leadership, the fragmented kingdoms were reunited, and Thais exerted more control over Cambodia and Laos. Taksin also brought northern Thailand into his kingdom. However, Taksin was forced to abdicate as king in 1782, when a revolt pushed him out of power, and he was later executed.

THE CHAKKRI DYNASTY

With the death of Taksin, the Thai throne fell to Chao Phraya Chakkri, who had played a leading role with Taksin in the military campaign against the Burmese. He was made king, renamed Rama I, and served as the first ruler in the era known as the Chakkri Dynasty. Rama I served as king from 1782 until 1809. He moved the capital to Bangkok, where it remains today, rebuilt the economy, and repulsed frequent Burmese attacks on Siam. The Chakkri Dynasty instituted the procedure of having royal descendents become king. Today, the king of Thailand is from the Chakkri lineage, a line that has continued unbroken since 1782.

The West again appeared on Thailand's doorstep in the early nineteenth century. In 1826, the British were victorious in Burma, but to avoid confrontation and establish a noncolonial relationship with the British, Nang Klao (also called Rama III) signed a trade and commerce agreement called the Burney Treaty in 1826. Later, in 1833, Rama III signed a similar agreement called the Treaty of Amity and Commerce with the United States. Rama I, II, and III were successful in moderating Western influence in Thailand, but the situation grew more difficult after the death of Rama III in 1851.

Mongkut was Nang Klao's half brother, and he succeeded to the throne after Rama III died. Mongkut was a Buddhist monk who, as king, became Rama IV. He ruled until 1868 and worked to clean up the Buddhist religion in Thailand. Over the years, the faith had picked up many superstitions and he wanted the religion to return to its original teachings. Mongkut also opened Thailand's doors to outside countries more than had his predecessors. Initiating another political tightrope walk, he believed that Thailand's chances of remaining independent would be strengthened by working with the European powers. He was aware that attempts to resist, such as had unsuccessfully been done in Burma and elsewhere in Asia, simply did not work. Mongkut and his son Chulalongkorn (called Rama V as king) worked to keep Siam independent by playing the British and French against each other. They also were forced to give up their claims to lands they had

Chulalongkorn, who is better known as Rama V, served as king of Siam from 1868 to 1910. In addition to Westernizing the country, Chulalongkorn abolished slavery and modernized both the government and education system.

controlled in Laos (1893), Cambodia (1907), and on the Malay Peninsula (1909).

Chulalongkorn created a situation in which Thailand became a buffer state (a neutral territory between two or more antagonistic powers) between the British in Burma and the French in Cambodia and other lands in the area called French Indochina (present-day Cambodia, Laos, and Vietnam). With this key positioning, Thailand stayed independent of Western rule. Chulalongkorn also modernized Siam's government and education system, and ended the practice of slavery. Trains and the telegraph were introduced during his reign. By 1897, tracks extended from Bangkok to Ayutthaya, and other lines were added soon after. Rama V died in 1910, and the date of his death, October 23, is still celebrated as a national holiday in Thailand.

Vajiravudh, Chulalongkorn's second son, succeeded his father in 1910 and was designated as Rama VI. He was a nationalist who had been educated in England. When World War I broke out, Vajiravudh sided with the Allies against Germany and declared war in 1917. This won Thailand some favor with both the French and British. Under the rule of Rama VI, Siam was also a founding member of the League of Nations in 1919. He ruled until his death in 1925 at the young age of 44 and was succeeded by his brother Prajadhipok (Rama VII).

THE CONSTITUTIONAL ERA

Prajadhipok was the youngest son of Chulalongkorn, and his route to the throne was a bit unorthodox. He was only 32 years old when he became king. He, like his brother, had been educated in England, but he was unprepared to serve as king, because his ascension was thought very unlikely. He was intelligent and established a body called the Supreme Council of the State to advise him on various matters. This made other civil servants jealous, and there was nearly a bloodless coup in 1932. A number of civil servants, representatives of the People's Party, and some army officers acted while the king was away at his summer retreat in Hua Hin. They arrested many of the princes and demanded that the king establish a constitutional monarchy with a democratic constitution. Prajadhipok agreed to the demands.

Pibul Songgram and Pridi Phanomyong were the leaders of the coup. Both had been educated in Europe. They and the others participating in the coup sought a more democratic government that would require the king to give up most political power, while retaining the symbolic importance of the monarchy. Parliamentary elections were held in November 1946 with Pridi and his liberal, pro-democracy party gaining favor. Pridi's opposition came primarily from a group led by Pibul, who had great support from the military. The groups favoring civilian or military rule had already staked out their positions within the fragile young constitutional government. This started a pattern that would result in the military taking over the government 17 times by 1992.

The swing between civilian and military rule in the twentieth century proceeded, while the monarchy stayed as a consistent factor that the Thai people looked toward for stability and hope. Prajadhipok had advocated for a constitutional government, but the 1932 coup happened before he could implement democratic reforms. In 1935, Prajadhipok abdicated the throne, because he could not accept the demands of nondemocratic forces that wanted to reduce royal power. Prajadhipok was an advocate of relinquishing royal powers to a civilian democratic government, but not to authoritarian interests that included the military. Today, Prajadhipok is credited as being Thailand's first strong advocate for a democratic government. His efforts added to the prestige of the throne and the royal family with the Thai people.

In 1939, the Kingdom of Siam became Thailand. By this time, the world was becoming increasingly unstable. Germany was beginning to gain strength in Europe, while, in Asia, Japan was moving aggressively to gain new territory and resources since it seized Manchuria (in present-day northeastern China) in 1931. Thailand's skill in walking political tightropes was tested once again as World War II burst into full fury. Pibal Songgram, a militarist, had become premier in 1938. He, like Japan, had expansionist yearnings. When the Japanese defeated the French during early fighting in Indochina, he linked Thailand to Japan's rising military power. With Japanese backing, Thailand was allowed to reclaim lands in Laos and Cambodia. However, with these territorial gains, Pibal also allowed the Japanese to enter Thailand. Pridi opposed this action. In 1942, under pressure from the Japanese, Pibal's government declared war on the United States and the United Kingdom. Amazingly, however, the Thai ambassador in Washington D.C., Seni Pramoj, refused to deliver the declaration of war! As a result, the United States never declared war on Thailand.

Even with Thailand allied with Japan, Pridi and Seni Pramoj worked closely with the United States to form an underground movement that opposed Japan. Increasingly, the Japanese viewed Thailand more as a colony than as an ally and this rightfully drew resentment from the Thai people. In 1944, Pibal was forced out of office, and a civilian government was established again. The country's name was reinstituted briefly as Siam, and in 1945, Seni became prime minister with the support of Pridi. However, Seni's leadership was short-lived. In 1947, Pibal staged a military coup after which the name Thailand was reintroduced.

The struggle between civilian and military rule has been a continuing saga for Thailand during the twentieth century. Military rule usually was ineffective, but civilian rulers would be removed from office whenever the military felt the government had fallen into disfavor. Pibal was often associated with the military rule, and Pridi with the civilian. Both leaders served as prime minister, and both played major roles in the country's governance during much of the twentieth century. Pibal's regime was ousted in another military coup in 1958 and he was forced into exile in Japan, where he died in 1964. Pridi tried to stage a revolution against Pibal's government in 1949, but it failed. He was forced into exile in China and later died in France in 1983. Both of these important figures in Thailand's twentieth-century history died in exile.

During the Vietnam War, U.S. troops used Thailand as a training ground and staging area for raids on North Vietnam. Pictured here are members of the 27th Infantry Division of the U.S. Army learning guerrilla warfare tactics near the northern Thailand town of Korat in preparation for the invasion by Pathet Lao Communist forces from Laos.

During the 1960s and 1970s, the Vietnam War had a considerable impact on Thailand. U.S. military forces used the country as a staging area for raids on North Vietnam. This brought a lot of money into Thailand, but it also served to fuel inflation. In 1967, Thailand was a founding member of the Association of Southeast Asian Nations (ASEAN). This organization helped the country to advance economically during the last decades of the twentieth century.

The decades of on and off military rule finally came to an end in 1992. In that year, citizens became disenchanted when the military-controlled government killed antigovernment demonstrators. A civilian prime minister was appointed by King Bhumibol Adulyadej, and elections were held in September 1992. Antimilitary political parties won the election and continued to serve through the end of the twentieth century. King Bhumibol (Rama IX) frequently stepped in, almost as a father figure, to calm conflicts when things appeared to be spinning out of control. Many citizens feared that the military would step in once more, continuing the revolving door of military and civilian governments.

One of the more serious problems that Thailand faced came in 1997 with the Asian financial crisis. The country tumbled into deep financial trouble because of speculation in real estate and corruption in government. In one week, the Thai currency, the Baht, plummeted 20 percent in value. The country eventually pulled out of the crisis, one that few Thais want to go through again. Thailand also adopted a new constitution in 1997. This document limited the influence of the military on government. It also institutionalized a number of progressive practices that had been introduced during the years since civilian government had been restored.

The twenty-first century has not been without problems. Muslim separatists have been operating in the southern part of Thailand, where the majority of the country's Muslims live, and separatists engaged in multiple raids and attacks in 2004 and 2005. To address the terrorist problem, Prime Minister Thaksin Shinawatra instituted emergency powers in July 2005. In addition, the west coast of Thailand was struck by a horrendous tsunami in December 2004. This tragic event killed an estimated 8,000 people in Thailand and left thousands homeless.

Corruption, particularly in government, also continued into the new century as billionaire Prime Minister Thaksin was indicted for fraud and tax evasion. These charges and popular discontent with his type of leadership caused him to announce in April 2006 that he would resign from office even though he had just won reelection three days earlier. After taking a brief leave of office, he returned to power and was the country's prime minister until September 2006.

Thailand has a unique history. Never colonized, it has worked an almost magical path between global powers that have had a presence in the region. It has made the transition from a kingdom to a constitutional monarchy. Governance has been plagued by corruption and a military that repeatedly interfered during the twentieth century. The king has often served as a long-term stabilizing factor by stepping in to keep various antagonistic players in line. Although it is a fragile democracy, Thailand has developed democratic traditions that may help it through the next crisis without military intervention.

People and Culture

A trip to Thailand leaves many fond memories, but there is one aspect of the country that is absolutely unforgettable—the Thai people and their fascinating culture. As one of the few countries in the world that is predominately Buddhist, the gentleness of this religion permeates the society. According to the CIA World Factbook, an overwhelming 94.6 percent of the population is Buddhist. With this vast majority, the religion strongly influences the way of life in Thailand today.

The culture also has a captivating language, which, when written, has a beauty that is visually artistic and, when spoken, is melodic to the ear. Look at the Thai characters for the phrase "nice to meet you," which is written as **ยินดีที่ได้รู้จัก**. Introduced in 1283 by King Ramkhamhaeng, the Thai language has a beauty that cannot be denied.

The arts and architecture of Thailand are similarly visually appealing. The dances performed by Thai women, with arched fingers and graceful movements that reflect years of study and practice, are unforgettable. Dances are performed to historical music with the exotic tunes and tones of Thailand. Huge statues of Buddha and majestic temples and buildings mark urban and rural areas with a distinctive flavor. Thai foods have now become a favorite throughout the world and are noted for their pungent spices and distinctive flavors.

However, in Thailand, there are human issues that have overshadowed the country's wonderful culture. Prostitution is an ongoing problem, one that is accompanied by an increasing incidence of HIV-AIDS and other sexually transmitted diseases. Women from the north are virtually sold by their families into prostitution in the south, so that the family can escape poverty. Thus, Thailand presents an extreme contrast between grinding poverty and the exotic and the beautiful. This chapter delves further into the culture and personality of Thailand and the core human elements that exist in the country.

CHARACTERISTICS OF THE PEOPLE

Ethnically, the country's population is quite homogeneous, with 75 percent being of Thai heritage, 14 percent being of Chinese heritage, and some 35 different ethnic groups making up the other 11 percent of the population. This figure includes Malay, Indians, and various indigenous hill tribe people. Measures of the quality of life in Thailand are generally higher than those of its neighbors. For example, nearly 93 percent of the population is literate. The per-capita gross domestic product (GDP) was estimated to be $8,300 in 2005. This figure is about $2,000 less than Thailand's southern neighbor Malaysia, but four times greater than neighbors Laos and Cambodia, and more than five times that of Myanmar. Workers are engaged in a variety of industries with 49 percent working in agriculture, 37 percent working in providing services, and 14 percent working in industry. Even with this relative prosperity, 10 percent of Thais still live below the poverty level.

Longevity of life for Thais is also relatively high when compared to neighboring Myanmar, Laos, and Cambodia. The life expectancy at birth is 72 years for Thais, with a projection of nearly 70 for men and just more than 74 for women. Thailand's population is about 65 million, and growing at a rate of about 0.7 percent each year, well below the world average of 1.2 percent.

BUDDHISM IN THAILAND

Buddhism, with its many beautiful temples and striking representations of Buddha, is readily evident on the Thai cultural landscape. It also permeates many aspects of society. Buddhism entered Thailand from India, where the faith began. India is where Buddha, known also by his birth name of Siddhartha Gautama, lived nearly 2,500 years ago. He was born in 566 B.C. to a wealthy family and led a very sheltered life in his younger years. At some point, he ventured outside of the walls of his palace and saw the shocking life outside. His trip beyond the walls revealed a world filled with the disease, poverty, and suffering that existed just outside his protected environment. The shock spurred him into a period of self-reflection in an effort to seek enlightenment. During this time, he went from his life of riches into a period where he led a very austere life and ate little.

After a long period of reflection and meditation, Gautama became enlightened at the age of 35 in the Indian city of Sarnath. His newfound wisdom showed him that neither the path of wealth nor poverty was the correct path. Instead, an individual should seek the middle road between self-indulgence and destitution. Thus, Buddhism is not really a religion; rather, it is a philosophy of life that contains specific teachings. Buddha is not regarded by Buddhists as being a God, but as an enlightened human. In fact, Buddhism does not recognize a god. It simply teaches that by following the teachings of Buddha, a person will lead a happier and more fulfilled life. Most Thai Buddhists follow the key teachings of Buddhism, which include the five fundamental precepts: not to harm or kill any living things; not to steal or take anything that is not freely given; to control sexual desires; not to tell lies; and not to drink alcohol or take drugs. By resisting these temptations and leading a good life, Buddha taught that followers could attain a state of Nirvana, a very desirable state that frees one from daily miseries and suffering. To achieve the state of Nirvana, Buddha advocated following the Eightfold Path, which teaches followers to believe right, desire right, think right, live right, do the right things, think the right thoughts, behave right, and practice deep reflection.

Theravada Buddhism became the official state religion of the Sukhothai Dynasty in 1238. This paved the way for Buddhism to grow in Thailand during the Ayutthaya era and to continue to prosper more than 800 years later. Theravada Buddhism is one of the many schools of Buddhist thought. Proponents claim that the beliefs of this school are closest to those that were originally taught by Buddha.

Tributes to Buddha abound in the country today. For example, there is the revered Temple of the Emerald Buddha in the Grand Palace in Bangkok. The city also houses the Temple of the Reclining Buddha at Wat Po, a 140-foot-long (43-meter) statue of Buddha, as well as a 5½ ton solid gold statue of Buddha at Wat Traimit. In the ancient ruins of Ayutthaya, there is a huge statue of Buddha called Phra Mangala Bophit. Monuments and temples are outward physical expressions of the philosophy that is held closely in the hearts, minds, and souls of Thailand's practicing Buddhists.

Another expression of faith is the Buddhist holidays that are celebrated in the country. Buddhist New Year is a three-day celebration following the first full moon in the month of April. Other holidays include Buddha's birthday and the first day of

More than 94 percent of Thailand's population consider themselves Buddhist, and the country's most sacred temple, Wat Phra Kaew, is on the grounds of Bangkok's Grand Palace. Pictured here is a procession of barges on the Chao Phraya River sailing past the Grand Palace during the celebration of King Bhumibol Adulyadej's fiftieth year on the throne in 1996.

Buddha's teaching. The frequency of Buddhist holidays and temples shows the widespread importance of the philosophy in the daily life of Thais today.

OTHER RELIGIONS IN THAILAND

Compared to Buddhism, all other faiths in Thailand are relatively minor. Islam and Christianity both exist in the country. Muslims live primarily in the south and in Bangkok. They make up 4.6 percent of the population, while Christians number less than 1 percent of the population.

Muslims follow the teachings of Muhammad, which are found in the Koran (Qu'ran). The five pillars of Islam provide the following core beliefs practiced by Muslims:

1. Profess a testimony of faith. Allah is the one true God.

2. Pray five times a day: at dawn, noon, midafternoon, sunset, and at night.

3. Give alms, which provide support to the needy.

4. Fast from dawn to sunset during the month of Ramadan.

5. Believers should take a pilgrimage to Mecca, Islam's holiest city, at least once during their lifetime.

Muslims constitute a majority of the population in the southern provinces, all of which are adjacent to Malaysia. Most of these Muslims are of Malay descent.

Muslims in the south often complain about discrimination and poverty. This and other complaints have fueled opposition to the government and the Buddhist majority in the country. This is also the region where Muslim extremists have carried out terrorist acts against the government. Attacks by Jemaah Islamiyah, an international terrorist group with connections to al-Qaeda, have become more frequent in Thailand during recent years.

Christians first came to Thailand in 1828. The religion never caught on well in the country. They often have been persecuted and have never received royal favor. Also, many people in the country believe that Christianity is "not Thai," which presents another obstacle to the faith's expansion in the country. Most of the Christians live in northern Thailand, where both Catholic and Protestant missionaries continue to work.

THAI LANGUAGE AND LITERATURE

The Thai language is one that is pleasing to both the eye and the ear. The beautiful, graceful curves of the written language cannot help but please the reader. At the same time, the tonal language of the Thais is almost musical with melodic tones that are very pleasant to the ear. Thai poets have often used this advantageous feature of the language to enhance the sounds of their poetry.

Thai is part of the Sino-Tibetan language family, but it has been influenced over time by other languages. The language has 44 consonants and 18 vowels. Tone marks are used in the written language to show how words are to be spoken. There are four major dialects of the Thai language. Each of these is spoken in the areas roughly equivalent to the four regions in the country as described in Chapter 2.

Thai writers use the visual and audio virtues of the language to enhance their literature. Much of the country's early literature was influenced by Indian traditions, such as the classic Thai story called *Ramakien*, which is a version of India's Hindu epic *Ramayana*. Religion tended to dominate early Thai literature until the nineteenth century, because earlier writings were written primarily by and for the aristocracy.

Thailand's greatest poet was Sunthorn Phu. He was born in 1786 and did most of his writing in the nineteenth century. He was a commoner poet who led a very colorful life. His writing became very popular, because he reflected the realities of daily life. He also wrote in a simple language that common people could understand. His most famous works were the *Phra Aphai Mani*, which he started writing while imprisoned for unruly behavior, and his nine travel accounts called the *Nirats*. He was a court poet for many kings and was later named Thailand's poet laureate. Thais continue to celebrate his birthday, June 26, with a holiday called Sunthorn Phu Day.

MUSIC AND DANCE

Early Thai music was passed on as an oral tradition until about 600 years ago, when it was recorded by written means. Early Thai groups were called *piphat* and usually included percussion instruments and woodwinds. Another type of music was called *khruang sai* and mainly used stringed instruments. Thai country music called *luk thung* developed in the middle of the twentieth century and remains popular today. Rural areas in the northeast still enjoy a local folk music called *mor lam*.

In the global world of entertainment, jazz and rock music have also found audiences in Thailand and both remain popular today. Thus, in Bangkok, one can hear a variety of musical forms, from the works of female singer Pumpuang Duangjan, who introduced electronic *luk thung*, to Western bands such as Green Day and U2.

Thai dance is an art form with strong ties to the country's history, culture, beliefs, and traditions. The monarch traditionally has given strong support to dance, and the art form remains very dynamic today. There are two major forms of dance in Thailand: folk dance and classical dance. Folk dances are different in each of the four different regions. They usually are tied to traditional daily activities such as working in the rice fields, or to religious celebrations. The names of dances, such as the Butterfly Dance, Fingernail Dance, or the Scarf Dance, reflect the simple themes.

Dancers perform in brilliant costumes that glitter with gold and other bright colors. The hand, arm, head, and leg positions of classical Thai dance are very intricate and performers can spend decades learning the proper movements and placement of fingers, arms, and legs. Classical dance has 108 different movements, and these positions are different for women and men. Some of the movements are gracefully hypnotic to watch, as hands curve backward in an arc and legs move gracefully in a style that is mesmerizing in its beauty.

THAI FOOD

Food is another of Thailand's cultural delights. Thai cuisine is unforgettable, with an array of subtle and not-so-subtle spices that both tantalize and please a taster's palate. The range of spices goes from hot and spicy to mellow and delicate. Spices and ingredients used in cooking include hot peppers, lime juice,

Folk and Classical are the two major forms of dance in Thailand and are an integral part of the country's culture. Dancers often perform in brilliant costumes that glitter with gold and other bright colors.

lemon grass, ground peanut, and black pepper. Ginger, coconut milk, coriander, garlic, sweet basil, mint, tomatoes, onion, and curry are also widely used. Many of these ingredients are blended together into tasty sauces that are combined with chicken, seafood, or beef and vegetables and served over a bed of rice.

Rice is eaten at nearly every meal and serves to balance some of the more spicy sauces. In the south, rice usually is steamed; however, in the north people prefer stickier rice. Unusual ingredients like crickets and various insect larvae are eaten in dishes in rural areas. Other exotic Thai foods include fried silkworm, eel, and animal parts like pork lungs. However, fish, pork, and chicken are more commonly served along with vegetables in the various tasty sauces featured in Thai cooking.

Thai cooking has become very popular around the world. Thai dishes like satay, chicken curry, pad thai (fried noodles), and hundreds of others have become common dishes outside of the country. For example, there is even a Web site (Thai-food.com) for people in the United States looking for Thai restaurants. Besides being delicious, most Thai foods are also very nutritious, still another factor adding to their worldwide popularity.

CURRENT ISSUES FACING THAI PEOPLE AND CULTURE

Some potentially critical challenges confront the Thai people. As noted previously, the issue of prostitution, which is officially illegal, remains a huge problem. Young women and men are drawn, or often pushed, into this seedy industry, creating social problems that include an increased incidence of sexually transmitted diseases such as HIV/AIDS.

HIV/AIDS first appeared in Thailand in 1984, where it initially was spread mainly by drug users. The sex industry was the next to be hit with the disease, as rates moved to epidemic proportions in some parts of the country. Fortunately, recent government efforts to curb the spread of HIV/AIDS have achieved better results than in many other less fortunate countries around the world. In 2003, it was estimated that 570,000 people in Thailand had HIV/AIDS, resulting in some 58,000 deaths that year. This figure represents nearly 1 percent of the country's population! The estimated rate of HIV/AIDS infection still stands at about 1½ percent, and there are many unreported cases in the country.

The issue of prostitution itself remains another cultural challenge in Thailand. Prostitution started to flourish in the 1960s, when the United States began to use Thailand as a rest and recreation base for troops who were engaged in the Vietnam War. In 1957, it is estimated that 20,000 prostitutes worked in Thailand. By 1964, the number had exploded to more than 400,000. Estimates on the number of prostitutes in the country today vary widely. Thailand's Public Health Department estimates that there are 75,000 prostitutes, whereas the magazine *The Nation* placed the number at 2.8 million in 2004.

The problem of prostitution is related to other problems facing women in Thailand. One study shows that the vast majority of female prostitutes in Bangkok come from rural areas, suggesting that the trafficking of women is also prevalent. Social inequality and fewer economic opportunities for women present a cultural issue that looms large for Thailand. Female literacy is about 4 percent less than for men, and men attain a higher average level of education. Some claim that the inferior status of women is tied to Buddhism and other cultural traditions. Many nongovernmental organizations remain concerned about this situation and are working with the government and Thai women to improve their status.

Thailand presents an enticing culture to investigate. From exotic foods and dances to fascinating music and literature, the country is blessed with cultural depth and complexity. Problems exist, but they should never prevent visitors from exploring the attractions and mysteries of Thailand.

5

Government and Politics

T he tradition of a monarchy stretches back more than 700 years in Thailand and forms a core and enduring element in the country's governance. Along with this royal heritage, Thailand has had a number of different ruling mechanisms that influence the politics and government of the nation today. From monarchy to military dictatorship to constitutional monarchy, Thailand has undergone huge transitions in governance, some of which happened in only a few years. Powerful kings, foreign intrusions, coup d'etats, and brief democratic periods checker Thailand's governmental history. These events provide a political heritage that helps us better understand the precarious nature of Thailand's government today.

A bloodless coup in 1932 transformed Thailand's government from an absolute monarchy to a constitutional monarchy. An absolute monarchy has a sovereign, a king or queen, whose power is not limited by laws or opposition groups. This is contrasted with a constitutional monarchy, such as that found in Thailand or the United Kingdom today. Under this system, responsibilities of the king or queen are spelled out in the constitution, in laws, and by customs. Though Thailand is a constitutional monarchy today, it has not always been, and the years since 1932 have presented a variety of governmental structures and challenges.

Thailand's haphazard path toward becoming a more democratic society is quite different from other nations in Southeast Asia. Others in the region were under European rule at some time in their history. For example, the French controlled much of Indochina, including Laos, Vietnam, and Cambodia, and the British controlled Malaysia, Burma (Myanmar), and Singapore for long periods. European influence on governance lingers today in many of the practices and institutions in these former colonies. As an example, Vietnam's Supreme People's Court, the country's highest court, still possesses some of its French colonial traditions in civil matters. Thailand, on the other hand, was never controlled by a colonial power that influenced its style of government. Thailand's path has been primarily chosen by tradition, the king, and the Thai people.

THAILAND'S CONSTITUTION

A constitution represents the highest law in democratic countries. Thailand's constitution may be challenged, however, if important players like the king or the military, or even terrorists in the south, are able to gather more power than provided for in the constitution. Unlike the constitution in the United States, Thailand's current constitution is relatively new. It was adopted on December 9, 1997. Commitment to the constitution may change from time to time in order to meet the needs of the day. This has happened before on many occasions in Thailand, as earlier constitutions simply were thrown out, avoided, or frequently changed. In fact, the country has had no fewer than 15 charters and constitutions since 1932!

Thailand's most recent constitution was adopted on December 9, 1997, and drafted to eliminate political corruption and provide citizens with more civil liberties. Pictured here are residents of Bangkok waving green flags in support of the draft charter of the constitution in September 1997. Tragically, the constitution was suspended in 2006 following a military coup.

There are many ways to test a constitution to determine how "democratic" it is. One way is to determine whether the document clearly provides for the rule of law over all people, including leaders, kings, and the military. If any individuals are not subject to the constitution or the laws of the country, it means that powerful and influential people can be more important than the laws. This situation is called the rule of man. The rule of man may work reasonably well if the leaders are benevolent. But this political structure can be a disaster if a despot rules with iron-handed force and objectionable practices in governance. With the rule of man, there are no guarantees for the people.

In democracies, political leaders serve their constituency. Constitutions in these societies allow citizens to speak freely,

assemble peacefully, and worship faiths of their choice. Dictatorships, where the rule of man prevails, represent another end
of the political spectrum where leaders are not directly subject
to the citizens. These regimes may be arbitrary and cruel, or
they may be kind and benevolent in their decisions. Public
policies (laws and administrative rulings) in a democracy are
subject to the consideration of citizens. This happens either
directly through mechanisms such as referendum elections or
indirectly through their elected representatives in the legislative
and executive branches.

Thailand's constitution seemingly makes the role of the
king and democracy confusing in the first sections of the document. In Chapter I, titled "General Provisions," the document
states the following:

> **Section 1.** Thailand is a unified and indivisible
> Kingdom.
>
> **Section 2.** Thailand adopts a democratic regime of
> government with the King as Head of State.
>
> **Section 3.** The sovereign power emanates from the
> Thai people. The King who is Head of State shall
> exercise such power through the National Assembly,
> the Council of Ministers and the Courts in accor-
> dance with the provisions of this Constitution.
>
> **Section 4.** The Thai people, irrespective of their birth
> or religion, shall enjoy equal protection under this
> Constitution.
>
> **Section 5.** The provision of any law, which is contrary
> to or inconsistent with this Constitution, shall be
> unenforceable.

At first glance, this section appears to place the king under
the rule of law in sections 2 and 3. However, Chapter II, titled,
"The King," muddies the issue by stating:

Section 6. The King shall be enthroned in a position of revered worship and shall not be violated. No person shall expose the King to any sort of accusation or action.

Section 7. The King is a Buddhist and Upholder of religions.

Section 8. The King holds the position of Head of the Thai Armed Forces.

Does the second part of section 6 place the king above the law? Will there truly be freedom of religion with section 7? Does the unelected king still remain the true power in the country as the head of the armed forces as stated in section 7? These and other questions face Thai citizens and their relatively new constitution.

Even with these questions, Thailand's 1997 constitution establishes the governmental institutions and procedures that have an impact today. The role of the king is very important, but more democratic institutions have also been created to govern the country.

THE KING

The king is mentioned frequently in Thailand's constitution. He has many important roles in governance and is head of state, which means that he is the symbol of Thailand's unity and national identity. The present king is His Majesty Bhumibol Adulyadej, King Rama IX of Thailand. He has been the king of Thailand since 1946, when he assumed the throne at the age of 18. He is the world's longest serving head of state. Surprisingly, King Bhumibol was born in the United States in 1927 in Cambridge, Massachusetts. Under his monarchy, he has played an active role in politics and government. In 1976, he even actively supported a return to military rule, and he has supported other military regimes at times. However, people

King Bhumibol Adulyadej ascended to the throne of Thailand on June 9, 1946, and is the longest-serving monarch in the world. Adulyadej is pictured here, in 2006, with his wife, Queen Sirikit, at the royal palace during the sixtieth anniversary of his coronation.

today view him as democracy's hero, because in 1992, he confronted the country's military leader, General Suchinda Kraprayoon, on national television and insisted that he resign.

The king is ever present in the daily life of the Thai people. He is pictured on signs and posters everywhere, and his image is on virtually all of the nation's coins, paper currency, and even postage stamps. King Bhumibol has played a very active role in the country's governance. This makes Thailand's status as a constitutional monarchy different than in most other countries of the world, where the role of monarch is mostly symbolic.

According to the constitution, the king must be a Buddhist, but he must uphold all faiths. Perhaps more importantly, he is the head of the Thai armed forces and has the power to declare war with the approval of the National Assembly. He also can declare and end martial law in the country. The king has the constitutional responsibility of appointing (or removing) the 18 members of the Privy Council who are responsible for advising him on his constitutional responsibilities. The oath of office for council members is interesting because of whom they pledge allegiance to:

> I, (name), do solemnly declare that I will be loyal to the King and will faithfully perform my duties in the interests of the country and of the people. I will also uphold and observe the Constitution of the Kingdom of Thailand in every respect.

With this oath, what happens if the constitution and the king are in opposition with one another? What responsibility does a member of the Privy Council honor?

The king also has the power to sign bills that have been passed by the National Assembly. If he does not sign a bill into law, the National Assembly can override with a two-thirds majority vote. Thus, the king has power over pending legislation similar to that of the president in many countries. The difference is that the king is not elected. The king also appoints judges and 48 other ministers, called the Council of Ministers. He also has the power to dissolve the House of Representatives and call for new elections. There is no question that the role of the king in governance is more than symbolic.

THE EXECUTIVE BRANCH OF GOVERNMENT

Day-to-day government operations are administered by Thailand's executive branch, which is led by the prime minister. The prime minister, appointed by the king, serves as the country's head of government. In this role, he is responsible for the political issues of governing the country. The prime minister is appointed by the king and comes from the ruling party or coalition. By tradition, the prime minister is usually the head of the majority party or coalition in the House of Representatives (the Sapha Phuthaen Ratsadon).

Also key in administering government in Thailand is the Council of Ministers, a body that serves as the cabinet. As noted previously, ministers on the council are appointed by the king and are responsible, along with the prime minister, for conducting the business of the national government and its various departments. Ministers must be at least 30 years of age and serve until their term ends or is dissolved by the king.

The ministries are quite similar to those found in the cabinets in other countries. Examples of ministerial departments in Thailand include agriculture, commerce, defense, education, finance, foreign affairs, and industry. There also are ministries of the interior, justice, labor and social welfare, public health, university affairs, and science, technology, and the environment. Each of these ministries is responsible for managing the government's work in the area of designated responsibility. For example, the Ministry of Education is responsible for overseeing the education of nearly 16 million Thais who are engaged in educational activities as students or staff. The department also oversees cultural and religious affairs for the country.

THE NATIONAL ASSEMBLY

The constitution also creates Thailand's legislative branch, which is collectively called the National Assembly. The National Assembly is bicameral, or composed of two houses: a Senate and House of Representatives. The 500-member House of Representatives, the more powerful body, is called the *Sapha Phuthaen Ratsadon.* The other body in the National Assembly is the 200-member Senate, or *Wuthisapha.* Members of both houses are elected by popular vote for four-year terms. The speaker of the House of Representatives also serves as the president of the entire National Assembly. Both the speaker of the House and the president of the Senate serve terms concurrent with the entire bodies, unless the king dissolves the House session.

Citizens over the age of 18 are eligible to vote in elections. However, a person must be at least 25 years of age to run as a candidate for the House of Representatives and at least 35 years of age to run for a seat in the Senate. Candidates must be a natural-born Thai citizen, which means they must have been born in Thailand.

Normal sessions of the National Assembly, called Ordinary Sessions by Thailand's constitution, last 90 days. There are two Ordinary Sessions each year. The length can be extended by the king if needed. Sessions can be shorter than 90 days, but only with the approval of the National Assembly. Bills may be introduced only by members of the House of Representatives or by members of the Council of Ministers. Finance bills may only be introduced in the House and must have the support of the prime minister. When a bill is passed by the House, it goes to the Senate, where the Senate can vote to approve the bill or send it back to the House. Disagreements are resolved by joint committees of the House and Senate.

Elections in February 2005 established the Thai Rak Thai Party (TRT) as the majority party, because it gained 60.66 percent of the popular vote. This resulted in the party winning

In 2005, Thaksin Shinawatra was overwhelmingly reelected prime minister of Thailand, winning more than 60 percent of the popular vote. More than 70 percent of Thais voted in the 2005 elections, the highest turnout in the country's history. Pictured here are Muslim voters in the southern province of Pattani.

377 of the 500 seats in the House of Representatives. The Democratic Party (DP) won 18.34 percent of the popular vote and claimed 96 seats in Parliament. The Chart Thai Party (TNP) received 11.39 percent of the popular vote and 25 seats. Finally, the Mahachon Party (PP) had 8.28 percent of the popular vote and won only 2 seats. The TRT party was led by telecommunications millionaire Thaksin Shinawatra, who won a decisive victory on a populist platform of encouraging economic growth and development. Thaksin Shinawatra also

served as Thailand's prime minister from 2001 until the coup d'etat in 2006.

THAILAND'S COURT SYSTEM

The court system is responsible for interpreting the laws of Thailand and determining guilt or responsibility in cases brought before them. The country's highest court is the Supreme Court, or *Sandika*, and its decisions are final. Judges on the court are appointed by the king as are other judges in Thailand. The Constitutional Tribunal is a separate entity from the Supreme Court, and it is solely responsible for determining whether laws are in conformance with Thailand's constitution.

Thailand's court system is divided into three tiers. The lowest courts are called Courts of First Instance and they are located around the country. The Courts of First Instance are divided into Provincial Juvenile and District Courts. These courts in Bangkok are divided even further into Civil, Criminal, Central Juvenile, Central Labor, Central Tax, and District Courts. In total, there are 135 First Instance Courts. The next-highest level court is the Court of Appeals. Thailand has one Court of Appeals in Bangkok and three other Courts of Appeals located in other areas of the country. The Supreme Court, the highest judicial body, represents the third tier in Thailand's court system.

PROVINCIAL AND LOCAL GOVERNMENTS

Since the 1997 constitution was implemented, Thailand has been working to decentralize power. These efforts imply that the central government is trying to move more responsibilities to local governments. Thailand has 76 provinces. Provinces are named after the region's capital city, and each, except the city of Songkhla, is the largest city in the province. Each of the provinces has a governor who is appointed by the Ministry of the Interior. Most of these governors are career civil servants. There is one exception to this policy and that is in Bangkok, where the governor is elected.

Each of the provincial governments is independent from the others, although the central government historically has exercised a large degree of control over all of the provinces. This direction comes from the Department of Local Administration, which is in the Ministry of the Interior. Thus, the process of decentralization runs counter to the long-standing practice of concentrating power in the hands of central government.

ROLE OF CITIZENS

Citizens in Thailand enjoy a variety of constitutional rights. Many of these are similar to other countries and the United Nations' Declaration of Human Rights. These include such rights as:

- Equality of all citizens under the law

- Protection of religious beliefs

- The right to a speedy investigation and trial and the right to legal assistance in criminal cases

- The right not to testify against oneself

- The right to own property

- The liberty to express opinions by speech, writing, and other forms of communication (although some limitations on these freedoms are listed in the constitution)

- The right to a primary education and standard health care

- The right to organize and form unions and associations

- The right to privacy

- Freedom of movement

Some of the rights of citizens have limitations or restrictions provided in the constitution. This may mean that the rights are not as clearly protected as in other countries, where court cases usually determine the boundaries of citizen rights.

Sectarian violence has been an ongoing problem in southern Thailand, where Islamic separatist groups and the Thai military have waged a battle that has been responsible for the death of more than 1,700 people since January 2004. Here, three Muslim students pass by a Thai soldier who is standing guard outside the Yala Islamic College in Yala Province.

Thai citizens also have various duties spelled out in the constitution. The first of these is "a duty to uphold the Nation, religions, the king and the democratic regime of government with the king as the Head of State according to this constitution." Other responsibilities of citizens are to:

- Participate in elections
- Defend the country
- Comply with the law
- Pay taxes
- Protect and maintain national arts and cultures

- Conserve natural resources and the environment as protected by the law

The newfound role of Thailand's citizens promises political freedoms and expects certain responsibilities. With few tests to the country's new constitutional record, human rights activists are watching the Thai government closely. They want to ensure that constitutional freedoms are actually protected and not violated by the practices of law enforcement and the courts. Unfortunately, Amnesty International has reported human rights violations against some Muslims in the south. Another violation is the restriction the government placed on media and foreign publications in 2002.

FOREIGN POLICY

Thailand is an active member of the world community. It is involved in a number of international organizations, including the United Nations, World Health Organization, Interpol, International Monetary Fund, and the World Trade Organization. It also holds active membership in ASEAN (the Association of Southeast Asian Nations), and United Nations Educational, Scientific and Cultural Organization (UNESCO), and many other groups. In addition to international organizations, Thailand has signed on to many important international agreements on issues such as biodiversity, climate change, desertification, endangered species, hazardous waste, marine life conservation, ozone layer protection, timber, and wetlands. Thailand is also a partner to the Kyoto Protocol on climate change.

Thailand's engagement in these activities clearly demonstrates that the country is a very active member of the international community with a wide variety of interests. Perhaps of greatest significance is Thailand's involvement in ASEAN. ASEAN has played a very significant role in the development of the country's economy. This organization will be discussed at length in Chapter 6's consideration of Thailand's economy.

This chapter has provided a snapshot of the important elements in Thailand's government. The role of the king and the military remain key political factors in the country's present and future. Thus, the precarious road to democracy in Thailand is paved on a heritage of royal power and influence. Will the king allow political dissent? What happens when the National Assembly overrides the king? Is there truly freedom of speech and the press if the king cannot be criticized? Many questions remain regarding Thailand's political future. In addition, the political directions of the country also color the nation's economic prospects. These economic prospects and scenarios are investigated in the following chapter.

CHAPTER

6

Thailand's Economy

Thailand's economy was one of the great surprises and success stories during the final decades of the twentieth century. The economies of Japan, South Korea, Singapore, Hong Kong, and Taiwan were sprinting forward during this time. Thailand's economy, on the other hand, seemed to be developing slowly. However, this image has rapidly changed, as the country has leaped forward with manufacturing and trade to build a modern and diverse economy.

Located on the dynamic Pacific Rim, Thailand has become a key member of the Association of Southeast Asian Nations (ASEAN) and a key trading partner with countries around the world. Even with its roots in agriculture, today, 45 percent of the country's economy comes from manufacturing and 46 percent from services. Agriculture today contributes only 9 percent of Thailand's gross domestic product (the GDP refers to the total amount of goods and services produced by a country within a calendar year). Nonetheless, nearly one of every two Thai workers is still employed in agriculture. In this context, you must remember that about two-thirds of the country's population is rural, and many people still are part of a traditional, subsistence-oriented folk culture.

While the Thai economy boomed over the 1980s and early 1990s, the growth came to a screeching halt when a currency crisis occurred in 1997 and 1998. Some major defaults in land payments and a number of major companies going out of business caused investors to panic. They sold their Thai currency, the Baht, for U.S. dollars and other more secure currencies. In four months, the Baht decreased in value by 40 percent against the dollar, mainly because the Thai government was slow in reacting to the developing economic crisis. Defaults on bank loans reached a staggering 18 percent in 1998, a dire situation that forced many financial institutions to close. Most countries in Southeast and East Asia were impacted by this financial crisis, but Thailand, Indonesia, and South Korea were hit hardest. In response, there was great political turmoil that eventually forced Thailand's leader, Prime Minister Chavalit Yongchaiyudh, to resign from office. The impact of the financial crisis continues to affect the country. In 1997, for example, the per-capita income in Thailand was $8,800 per year. During the crisis, it declined significantly and by 2006 had only recovered to about $8,500.

Fortunately, a number of lessons were learned because of the difficulties created by the financial crisis of 1997 and 1998. Transparency and openness of financial dealings has improved significantly, along with a tightening of monetary policy. In addition, there has been an improvement in the regulation of the banking and financial sectors of the economy. Another area of improvement has been the breaking of many "sweetheart" arrangements between government and business that were a form of corruption. These special deals created a marketplace that was often inefficient with costs being above what a truly competitive environment might bring.

Rubber is one of Thailand's most important crops and primary export commodities. According to the World Trade Organization, Thailand is the world's leading producer of rubber, generating more than 2 million tons a year. Pictured here is a rubber tapper transporting latex on her motorcycle in Yala Province.

AGRICULTURE

For centuries, agriculture served as the backbone of Thailand's economy, with rice long being the most important crop. However, the importance of agriculture has changed during recent years as other economic areas of activity, such as manufacturing, domestic trade, and services have expanded greatly. Rice-growing and other agricultural activities continue to employ nearly half of the country's labor force. But, as noted previously, it generates a small percentage of the country's GDP. Even though agriculture now plays a declining role in Thailand's economy, it is still very important. Rice remains the most important crop. In fact, the country raises so much of this nutritious grain that it has become an exporter of rice. Other major crops include rubber, corn, sugarcane, coconuts, soybeans, mung beans, peanuts, and cassava (a plant used to prepare tapioca).

Animal production is also important to Thailand's economy. The country is a big poultry producer; in 2003, Thailand produced 7 percent of all poultry meat traded in the global marketplace. However, this aspect of the country's economy is greatly threatened by the onset of the potentially deadly avian influenza. This disease has affected many countries in Southeast Asia, and tens of millions of birds have been culled (killed) to curb the spread of the virus. Poultry production in the country primarily includes chickens and ducks, which are used for both meat and eggs. Other animals produced include dairy cattle, pigs, water buffalo, and beef cattle for meat production.

MANUFACTURING

The importance of manufacturing has grown rapidly in Thailand. In fact, it was a major contributor to Thailand's rapid economic growth before the onset of the financial crisis. Much of the manufacturing in Thailand is intended for foreign markets. Among these goods are agricultural products, beverages, and tobacco products. Manufactured goods include cement, jewelry, electrical appliances and components, computers and parts, and integrated circuits. Other products include clothing and footwear, furniture, and plastics. Automobile production and the manufacture of car parts also have become very important. Companies with factories in Thailand include many of the world's major automobile producers, such as Ford, General Motors, Toyota, Mazda, and Mitsubishi.

The textile industry is also an important Thai industry, with a wide variety of products being manufactured. Among these are garments such as sportswear, sleepwear, suits, jogging suits, T-shirts, and even knitted clothing. Western companies such as Kimberly-Clark and Scott manufacture paper products like Kleenex and Huggies in Thailand, while several

Japanese companies manufacture products like air condition-
ers. Although only 14 percent of the workforce is engaged in
manufacturing, this sector contributes greatly to Thailand's
economy: More than 45 cents of every dollar in the Thai economy is generated by manufacturing.

TOURISM

The infectious courtesy, hospitality, and graciousness of the
Thai people make them great hosts for tourists venturing into
this part of Southeast Asia. The warmth of the people serves as
the best backdrop for this country's rich cultural heritage. Millions of people have visited Thailand and have returned home
with wonderful stories about the Golden Temple, beautiful
coastlines as found in Phuket and Pattaya, and historic locations like Ayutthaya, which has been designated by UNESCO as
a World Heritage Site.

Tourism is a major industry for Thailand, generating more
than $6 billion each year in revenue. This figure exceeds most
of Thailand's major exports and creates jobs for tens of thousands of Thai workers in many places around the country. In
areas such as coastal Phuket, tourism represents the primary
driving force for the economy.

Sadly, the country's tourism also has a seamy side, because
of the rampant prostitution that exists in the country. This
industry regularly spawns sex tours from Western countries,
the Middle East, and East Asia, allowing foreigners to prey on
young men and women who are forced into prostitution. As
you might expect, HIV-AIDS rates are quite high, and many
in this industry have become infected with this and other sexually transmitted diseases. The government is working to
decrease this sector of the economy, because prostitution is
illegal. The poverty that contributes to prostitution has been
difficult to break. As a result, places like Bangkok and other
tourist destinations such as Pattaya still harbor this industry.
Thailand was the first country in Southeast Asia to be struck

by AIDS, and today about 1.5 percent of the adult population is infected with HIV-AIDS. Public efforts are having some success in reducing this often-deadly disease, and other efforts to eliminate the sex tourism industry are showing some signs of progress.

Anyone visiting Thailand as a tourist will be pleased and perhaps somewhat surprised. It is an incredible country filled with wonderfully welcoming people, world-class accommodations, fantastic foods, and fascinating places to visit. The gentleness of the people and the culture make a visitor feel very welcome and safe. Traditional dances and costumes are alive with movement and color. Buddha serves as a constant and peaceful reminder of the country's religious heritage. Temples, called *Wat*, are located throughout the country, and many of these beautiful structures attract curious visitors. A visit to Thailand is an unforgettable experience, and tourism leaves the coffers of the Thai economy a bit richer.

NATURAL RESOURCES

Thailand is a country blessed with a wealth of varied natural resources. These resources, combined with a productive workforce, provide an important foundation for manufacturing and a diversified economy. Some of the important mineral resources include tin, tungsten, tantalum, lead, and fluorite. Thailand is among the top three world producers of tungsten and tin. Mineral fuels include lignite coal and natural gas. There is abundant timber to produce lumber and paper products, and trees that produce natural rubber. Rivers and seas produce a variety of fish, shrimp, and other marine life. The country also has good lands for farming.

Thailand produces some oil, but must import much of its needed supply. Proven oil reserves are less than 600 million barrels. Extensive oil exploration is being conducted in the country, and there appear to be some promising developments offshore in the Gulf of Thailand. The country's oil industry giant is PTT, which was formerly called the Petroleum Authority of Thailand. The government owns two-thirds of this company.

Natural gas is used to produce much of the country's electricity. Even though Thailand is about 80 percent self-sufficient in terms of its natural gas needs, the growth of demand is increasing at about 5 to 6 percent per year. Thailand's largest natural gas field is at Bongkot, which is located 400 miles (644 kilometers) south of Bangkok in the Gulf of Thailand. Additional natural gas is being piped in from Myanmar, Thailand's neighbor to the west. Unocal is the largest producer of Thai natural gas, with Chevron Texaco also a leading producer.

GETTING AROUND IN THAILAND

Transportation facilities are relatively easy to find in Thailand. The country has a number of different systems that help people move efficiently from one destination to another. Thailand's role as Southeast Asia's number-one travel destination certainly has been a factor in developing and maintaining efficient transportation systems. For example, a traveler will usually enter the country via Bangkok International Airport. This modern facility handles 30 million passengers each year. More than 80 airlines serve the city and connect Thailand to most of the world's great cities. Bangkok's airport is one of the busiest in the world for passenger traffic and cargo handling.

Bangkok is not the only important city for air transportation in the country. Others cater to tourists or serve as regional airline hubs for Thais. Phuket International Airport is the second-busiest passenger and cargo facility in the country, serving millions of passengers, most of them tourists. Chiang Mai International Airport serves as a gateway to northern Thailand, while Hat Yai International Airport is a gateway to the south. Other important air hubs are the airports at Suvarnabhumi and Chiang Rai.

Thailand also possesses efficient bus and rail systems. Bangkok is the hub for both of these transportation systems,

Bangkok's Sky Train opened in 1999 and has alleviated some of the city's traffic congestion. There are currently 23 stations along the system's 14.3-mile (23-kilometer) route, and more than 500,000 single trips are made each day on the line.

which fan outward from the city. In addition to being the national center of bus and train systems, Bangkok also has excellent urban bus and train service. Newest of the urban systems is the Sky Train, which opened in 1999. The congested streets of Bangkok can make traveling by bus, truck, or car extremely slow and so the Sky Train operates as an elevated rail system to avoid the traffic. The city also has a subway system, and some water transportation is available that can carry the traveler to Malaysia, China, Laos, or Myanmar.

A novelty of Bangkok's streets is the *tuk-tuk*. This three-wheeled vehicle operates much like a car, but has only three wheels. These vehicles are loud, somewhat unsafe, and produce a trail of smoke when they accelerate. For years, Thais have tried to ban the vehicles, but they remain on the streets today as a cheap means of transportation that are popular with tourists. Bicycles are commonly used outside of Bangkok and there are even tuk-tuks without motors.

Located between the Gulf of Thailand (which is connected to the Pacific Ocean) and the Indian Ocean, Thailand also has a number of important ports. Bangkok, Laem Chabang, Prachuap, and Si Racha all possess ports of some importance to the country. The two most important ports are at Bangkok and Laem Chabang, where the harbors are deep enough to accommodate both cruise and cargo ships.

COMMUNICATION

Thailand operates a number of the communication systems common to most nations. The postal system is very efficient in Thailand, and the country is known for its large and colorful stamps. Until 2006, the phone system was under public ownership, but since that time, private companies have been allowed to operate. The phone system is very efficient and modern, with nearly 7 million Thais having land-based lines and a whopping 27 million people (about 40 percent of the population) having cell phones. The country also has nearly 8 million Internet users and more than 100,000 Internet hosts.

Mass communication is also very modern in Thailand, which has more than 500 AM and FM radio stations. The television industry is centered in Bangkok, where six major stations dominate this medium. More than 80 percent of Thais report that television is their main source of news. Private ownership of the media is unusual. The Royal Thai Army owns channels 5 and 7, and the government controls most of the other stations. The sole exception is ITV, which is operated by the Shin Corporation, a large communications company. Much of the U.S. programming is disappearing from Thai stations, because viewers prefer programs that feature more local language and customs rather than the subtitled television series from overseas.

Thailand also has many newspapers, including *Thai Rath*, the country's most respected paper, which has a daily circulation of more than 1 million. Other important daily newspapers include the *Daily News*, *Kom Chad Leuk*, and *Khao Sod*. English-language newspapers like the *Bangkok Post* and *The Nation* are also available in urban areas. All of the major newspapers, except for one in Chiang Mai, are published in Bangkok and distributed around the country. Freedom of the press is guaranteed by Thailand's constitution, but is practiced more actively in newspapers than by television. Even though newspapers are not supervised as closely as television, it is widely believed that the practice of self-censorship is often conducted by management. Nevertheless, the newspapers in Thailand are probably the least censored in Southeast Asia.

FOREIGN TRADE AND ASEAN

Thailand has become a trading giant in recent years. The country touches the world with its quality products and with import needs. To enhance and develop its role as a trading country, Thailand was a founding member of the Association of Southeast Asian Nations (ASEAN). This organization was founded in 1967 by Indonesia, Malaysia, Singapore, the Philippines, and Thailand. Subsequently, Brunei Darussalam joined in 1984, Vietnam in 1995, Laos and Myanmar in 1997, and Cambodia in 1999.

The stated objectives for ASEAN reveal not only the economic role of the organization but other important regional and global aims:

> The ASEAN Declaration states that the aims and purposes of the Association are: (1) to accelerate the economic growth, social progress and cultural development in the region through joint endeavors in the spirit of equality and partnership in order to strengthen the foundation for a prosperous and peaceful community of

Southeast Asian nations, and (2) to promote regional peace and stability through abiding respect for justice and the rule of law in the relationship among countries in the region and adherence to the principles of the United Nations Charter.

While the economic relationships created by the ASEAN charter document are listed first, the second aim extends the organization into a variety of other areas. The economic foundation is leading member countries toward economic integration.

ASEAN is not the only economic organization with which Thailand is affiliated. The country also is a member of the Asia-Pacific Economic Cooperation (APEC), Economic and Social Commission for Asia and the Pacific (ESCAP), the Asia-Europe Meeting (ASEM), World Intellectual Property Organization (WIPO), International Monetary Fund (IMF), the World Trade Organization (WTO), and other economic forums. All of these international economic relationships underscore the importance of trade to Thailand.

Thailand's leading partners for its exports, in order of importance, are the United States, Japan, China, Singapore, Malaysia, and Hong Kong. Japan is the leading source of imports, followed by China, the United States, Malaysia, Singapore, Taiwan, and the United Arab Emirates (UAE), which is a major source for Thailand's imported oil.

A TIGER STILL IN THE MAKING?

Collectively, Hong Kong, Singapore, South Korea, and Taiwan were referred to as the "Four Tigers" or "Four Dragons" in the 1980s because of their rapid economic growth. During the late 1980s, Thailand was looking like a fifth tiger, when economic growth rocketed forward at a rate of more than 12 percent. This expansion stunned many in the West, who believed that Thailand was not equipped for this rapid economic growth. Annual economic growth in the country has decreased to around 4½ percent as a result of the recent financial crisis, but this is still a rate that exceeds that of most countries in the world.

Thailand is fortunate in that it has a diversified economy. No one segment dominates, and agriculture, manufacturing, tourism, services, and natural resources all contribute to the country's economic prosperity. Abundant resources including fish, oil, and natural gas are found in the seas surrounding Thailand. The country produces foods to feed itself and has become an exporter of rice. It also continues to develop new sources of energy. The primary challenges facing the country from an economic standpoint are in the area of environmental degradation. Developing a stable economy and a sustainable environment is a vitally important balancing act that Thais will continue to face in the twenty-first century.

7

Major Urban Areas in Thailand

Bangkok is the city that most people think of when discussions focus on Thailand. There is no doubt that Bangkok is a significant world-class city and one that we will explore in this chapter. But there are other cities in Thailand that also have regional, national, and international importance. Chiang Mai, Phuket, Phitsanulok, Chiang Rai, Lamphun, Lampang, Mae Hong Son, Khorat, and Sukhothai are just a few of these urban centers. This chapter investigates one city in each of the four major regions of Thailand in order to provide an expanded examination of the character of the city and region within which it is located.

Like most visitors to Thailand, our first stop will be at the great city of Bangkok in the central region. Later sections will examine Chiang Mai in the northern region, Nakhon Ratchasima in the Khorat Plateau region, and Phuket in the southern region.

BANGKOK: THE CAPITAL CITY

According to the *Guinness Book of World Records*, Bangkok's full name is the world's longest place name. The city was named by King Rama I, and the long version is Krungthep mahanakon boworn ratanakosin mahintarayudyaya mahadilop noparata-narajthani burirom udomrajniwesmahasatarn amornpimarn avatasatit sakattiyavisanukamphrasit. The long name actually provides a brief history of the city, but for our purposes, it will be translated as "City of Angels."

Bangkok is by far the largest city in Thailand, with a population that the United Nations estimated in 2003 to be more than 6,500,000 people. Another 3 million people live in adjacent communities, to create a metropolitan population of about 10 million, or about the size of Chicago, Illinois, and its suburbs. This population is many times greater than that of the country's second-largest city. Bangkok is both teeming with activity and choked with traffic and pollution. People from around the country migrate to the city in search of work. This factor contributes to a critical shortage of housing and creates a host of other social problems.

Bangkok is also the city that houses the national capitol, and the major functions of government are centered here. The Parliament building is somewhat visually surprising. The structure looks like it would be more at home in a Western country than in Bangkok. This anomaly aside, Bangkok is well known for its fascinating Thai architecture.

King Rama I established his capital here, on the floodplain delta of the Chao Phraya River, in 1782. He built the Temple of the Emerald Buddha (Wat Phra Kaew) and the Grand Palace (Wat Po). Since its very beginning, the city has also served as the primary home of the monarch and royal family. The Chao Phraya River also feeds the city's many canals, which led to Bangkok's nickname as the "Venice of the East."

Traffic problems, for which the city is infamous, are being addressed with a new mass transit system. Among these are the

Among the major environmental concerns in Bangkok is the unsanitary water, which has largely been caused by industrial pollution. Although the government has recently made a concerted effort to clean up Bangkok's canals, many of the city's waterways, such as this one, are brackish and dangerously polluted.

Sky Train and a subway system, both of which have helped, although not completely solved, the traffic issue. Other problems that face the city include water and air pollution. Of course, there are other challenges facing the city. Among these are prostitution, underage drinking, widespread drug use, and rampant venereal disease. Unsanitary water means that tourists should drink only bottled water and to use bottled water to brush their teeth. Even with these many and varied challenges, traffic remains the city's greatest and seemingly most insurmountable problem.

Bangkok is the financial center for Thailand, a role it is quickly claiming for all of Indochina. Hundreds of financial and business interests have headquarters in the city, resulting in modern, beautiful buildings marking the skyline. World-class hotels also are available, and shoppers are treated to many fine facilities where the goods of the country and the world can be found. Examples of both popular and traditional folk culture are available for residents and tourists alike. Sights range from the Grand Palace and traditional dance performances to water-parks, zoos, and even a Thai doll museum.

As noted previously, Bangkok serves as a major air destination and hub for Asia. More than 30 million passengers travel to or through Bangkok International Airport (BIA) annually. BIA also is shared with the Royal Thai Air Force's Don Muang Royal Thai Air Force Base, which mainly uses the facility for noncombat aircraft. A new airport, Suvarnabhumi, or New Bangkok International Airport (NBIA), opened on September 28, 2006. The facility had been under construction for years, however, and originally was set to open in 2005. The new airport inherited the international traffic from BIA. Its terminal is the world's largest, and its control tower—at 433 feet (132 meters)—is the world's highest.

Bangkok is also a major port city. The city's port is called Klong Toey Port, and it connects easily to both road and rail systems. These systems carry goods to and from other areas in the country, and carry Thai goods and products out for export. However, Laem Chabang Port, 90 miles south of Bangkok, is quickly becoming the more modern and accessible international port for Thailand. Presently, Klong Toey and Laem Chabang ports each handle about 45 percent of the containers that arrive, with the remaining 10 percent passing through the port of Songkhla.

CHIANG MAI: GATEWAY TO THE NORTH

Chiang Mai is Thailand's second-largest city, with a population of about 700,000 (there are 1.6 million people in the entire Chiang Mai Province). The city, located about 460 miles (750 kilometers) northwest of Bangkok, was established in 1296 and celebrated its seven hundredth anniversary in 1996. The settlement originally was built on the Ping River, which is an important tributary of the Chao Phraya River. In 1558, it was conquered by Burma and remained under Burmese rule until it was liberated in 1774 by King Taksin. The city was actually deserted for 15 years from 1776 to 1791, as a result of successive wars with Burma. But like the legendary phoenix bird, the city rose again.

The city serves as a gateway to the northern region, which has a bounty of attractive tourist sites. With Thailand's largest zoo, beautiful mountains, parks, and fascinating hill country cultures, the region presents many options. This, combined with easy domestic travel, makes the fast-growing city both a regional and international transportation hub. Chiang Mai International Airport is one of the five international airports in the country. The airport serves nine airlines and accommodates about 2 million passengers annually. The city is also a rail and bus hub.

Chiang Mai is home to more than 300 temples. Wat Chiang Man was built by King Mengrai in 1296 and is the city's oldest temple. The legendary Wat Phra That Doi Suthep Temple, with its special bells, was built in 1383. This beautiful temple is only 9 miles (15 kilometers) from the city and is named for the mountain on which it is located, Doi Suthep. An incredible view of Chiang Mai can be seen from the temple.

The nearby forests provide materials for artists who create elaborate and beautiful wooden carvings and other products. Chiang Mai also produces furniture, lacquer ware, silverware, bronze work, and other handicrafts like paper umbrellas, silk, and other textile products. Other products from the nearby Golden Triangle have tarnished the city's past, as the opium trade flowed through the region. Government efforts to curtail this production have met with more success in recent years, but the problem still exists.

NAKHON RATCHASIMA: GATEWAY TO THE NORTHEAST

Nakhon Ratchasima, generally known as Khorat, is Thailand's third-largest city, with a population approaching 500,000 people. The city is located 155 miles (250 kilometers) northeast of Bangkok in the western edge of the Khorat Plateau. It is the capital of the Nakhon Ratchasima Province and a regional air, highway, and railroad crossroads and hub.

Khorat is located in an agricultural region on the plateau and many of the products are shipped through the city on their way to markets. Among the chief crops grown in the region are rice, corn, and tobacco. There is also a substantial livestock industry. Copper is also mined nearby the city. Pottery is a major manufactured product. These, combined with government and regional financial, communication, and transportation systems, comprise the main elements of the economy.

This region also is filled with many sites for visitors. There are national parks and Khmer temples similar in style to Angkor Wat in nearby Cambodia. The region as a whole has a generous number of older Khmer sites. In Khorat, the Monument of Thao Suranari was erected in 1934 in honor of Khun Ying Mo, a woman who led a successful effort in 1826 to save the city from a Laotian invasion. A special celebration is held each year from March 23 to April 3 to recognize and honor her bravery.

Khorat also has a past that is tied to the U.S. military. During the years of the Vietnam War (1962–1975), the Royal Thai Air Force base served as a U.S. Air Force operations center. The base, located about five miles (eight kilometers) south of the city, continues to operate today.

PHUKET: PEARL OF THE ANDAMAN

Located about 500 miles (800 kilometers) south of Bangkok is the island and town of Phuket. Phuket is the largest island in

The Monument of Thao Suranari (pictured here) was erected in the town of Khorat in 1934 to honor Khun Ying Mo. As the story goes, Ying Mo and half the town's garrison protected the city from a Laotian invasion after her husband, the deputy governor, took the other half of the garrison to meet King Rama III.

Thailand. It is sometimes called the "Pearl of the Andaman," because the beautiful island is located in the Andaman Sea within the Indian Ocean. Phuket is a magnet for tourists from around the world. Glistening white sand beaches and picturesque rocky limestone cliffs provide sights that are unmatched. In addition, two-thirds of the island is covered by mountains and forests that add to the visual splendor.

Phuket is located in the Andaman Sea, off the southern coast of Thailand. The inviting tourist destination is a tropical paradise, with white sandy beaches and azure blue water.

Phuket was elevated to the status of a town in 1850, but the area had a long and eventful history before that time. Geologists suggest that the island was originally a cape that stretched into the Andaman Sea from the peninsula. Gradually, the island formed as it became detached from the mainland. Traders from around Asia often sought refuge on the island when storms struck. Phuket welcomed European travelers as early as the sixteenth century, and over time, Dutch, English, Portuguese, and French traders came to the area. Today, the town has grown rapidly to become a city of more than 250,000, with 1.6 million people on the entire island.

Two bridges connect the island and city to mainland Phang Nga Province. Phuket International Airport serves the town and island and is the second-busiest airport in the country for both passengers and cargo. Nearly three million passengers, primarily tourists, fly in and out of Phuket each year.

The island's economy, including lodging, restaurants, guide services, travel agencies, souvenir sales, fishing charters, and transportation, depends primarily upon tourism. The economy is not totally dependent upon tourism, however. There is an important agricultural component to Phuket's economy. Cashews, coconuts, and pineapples are grown, as are rubber-producing trees. Shrimp and pearl farming are important industries, along with traditional fishing and fish processing.

Phuket was badly damaged by the December 26, 2004, tsunami, which struck the island with deadly force. The toll included 262 people, about 40 percent of whom were tourists. The tsunami, which also struck other parts of peninsular Thailand, accelerated efforts to develop a tsunami early-warning system. The loss of life in Phuket was lessened by the numerous high-rise buildings, where people were able to seek refuge. Other areas on the peninsula had much greater loss of life, because the buildings were lower and offered much less protection to people. In all, there were 5,291 recorded deaths in Thailand resulting from the tsunami and about 4,000 people are still missing. Estimates are that 8,000 to 9,000 people perished in this tragic natural disaster. The tsunami also damaged the economy, as tourists have been slow to return to Phuket after the disaster and the fishing industry has been slow to recover.

Thailand, of course, has many other cities. Those included in this chapter not only have their own personality, but also reflect the region in which each is located. Each is a regional crossroad for economic, social, and political activity, with Bangkok being the hub of the nation. The importance of these cities to the surrounding rural areas is undisputed, as they help to connect regions, provinces, localities, and the country as a whole together.

8

Thailand Looks Ahead

T he twentieth century represents a tremendous transition in
the course of Thailand's history. The name of the country
changed from the Kingdom of Siam to Thailand, but other
changes involved much more than a change of name. During the past
century, Thailand moved from being an ancient kingdom, with historic roots in Ayutthaya and Bangkok, to a modern society marked
by modern cities and regional leadership in Southeast Asia.

Thailand's future is difficult to gauge, because predictions can
be based on many different scenarios. While the future tends to be
somewhat of a logical transition from the past and present, this
isn't always the case, and wars or revolutions can break out, or natural disasters like the 2004 tsunami can strike without warning.
Much like a river that seeks lower ground, this chapter will follow
the river of history and see what course the country may take in the
years ahead.

One of the greatest surprises of the last couple decades of the twentieth century was the rapid economic advance of Thailand. Before this, Thai kings had often been the inspiration and force behind the advancement of Thailand. For example, when King Rama V (Chulalongkorn) visited Europe right before the twentieth century, he came back to begin efforts to modernize Siam by initiating train service and the telegraph. He also instituted new sanitation and industrial practices. Rama VII (Prajadhipok) provides another example in his advocacy for a constitutional government in 1932. King Rama IX (Bhumibol), the present king, has continued to provide enlightened leadership, as he helped to return democracy to Thailand in 1992.

On numerous occasions, the monarchy helped to stabilize the country. The revolving-door relationship between military and civilian governments has often been pacified by the king, who has tremendous influence over the people. Respect for the king has been earned, but truly democratic societies also question authority. This is less likely to happen with the king in Thailand than in other democracies. Thus, the possibility remains that a king could abuse his power and threaten democratic practices in the country.

An optimistic element in Thailand's future is the Association of Southeast Asian Nations (ASEAN). This organization has expanded from the original five countries (Thailand, Philippines, Singapore, Malaysia, and Indonesia) to 10 members, as Brunei, Vietnam, Laos, Myanmar, and Cambodia have since joined. ASEAN has drastically increased and improved not only regional economic efforts, but also links the members in education, environment, and social endeavors. All of these efforts provide promise of a more integrated future and also provide vital support for regional stability and conflict reduction.

Tourism will likely remain a major contributor to the Thai economy, along with manufacturing, agriculture, and other services. However, the fragile nature of tourism became evident with the decreases that took place after the 2004 tsunami. The possibility of more attacks by militant Islamic terrorists in the south of Thailand might also threaten tourism and the Thai government. Thus, the government has worked with other ASEAN members to curtail the activities of Jemaah Islamiyah, a group connected to al-Qaeda. This group and others also have separatist intentions in the four southern, Muslim-dominated provinces. Because of the al-Qaeda connection to Jemaah Islamiyah, the United States and Thailand have been working more closely together on the war on terror in the country.

Other challenges, ranging from the traffic problems and pollution in Bangkok and other cities to social issues like prostitution and HIV/AIDS, also face Thailand. The potential for human-transmitted avian flu is also strongly present in Southeast Asia. People in Thailand have already been directly infected from birds with the avian-flu virus, and many of them have died. ASEAN is working on this issue. Member countries are investigating vaccines that can be used for immunization against this disease that already has killed hundreds of people in this part of the world.

Environmental issues certainly will continue to be a major source of concern and attention. Water and air pollution have reached the critical point in many locations, and deforestation has been a long-standing problem. Drug production continues in the Golden Triangle, but the government's crackdowns have had a positive impact. Drug use is also a problem, but penalties are severe, and offenders can be sentenced to life imprisonment, or even to death. In 2002, for example, Thai jails held more than 180 people who were awaiting execution on drug-related offenses.

Corruption continues to be an important issue in Thailand. Much of the corruption has deep historical roots. For example, government bureaucrats have long expected and received bribes for favorable decisions, and politicians have long attempted to buy votes. The 1997 constitution provides for better controls over corruption. One of these provisions

The first reported death from the avian flu occurred in Thailand in January 2004, and through the end of 2006, 17 people have died from being infected by the H5N1 virus. Thailand is one of the world's largest chicken exporters, but officials have had to destroy thousands of chickens to stop the spread of the disease.

allows citizens to have access to public information. Use of this right and other laws may reduce the corruption now present and increase governmental honesty.

Perhaps Thailand's greatest strength is its people. The people and their culture are truly unforgettable to visitors. Thailand

On September 19, 2006, the Royal Thai Army, under the command of General Sonthi Boonyaratkalin, led a military coup that ousted Prime Minister Thaksin Shinawatra. A new prime minister, Surayud Chulanont, was sworn in October 1, despite condemnation from foreign governments. Pictured here are tanks lining the streets just outside Bangkok, 36 hours after the coup.

is known as "the land of smiles," and this statement is completely true to anyone who has visited the country. Thais are excellent hosts, with a kindness and politeness that pervades the culture. In addition, literacy rates are high and the society is very cooperative, because less emphasis is placed on the individual than is found in Western societies. These are traits that bode well for both visitors and potential foreign investors who want to work within the country.

The people are also the key to Thailand's democratic future. As citizens, they have key responsibilities to watch over their government. Citizens are ultimately the final watchdog in democracies, and Thai citizens do not have experiences from a long democratic history to draw upon for guidance. However, the skepticism that citizens exhibited over possible conflicts of interest by Prime Minister Thaksin in 2005–2006 provides a positive template for the future. Thousands of demonstrators took to the streets to draw attention to their belief that the prime minister had abused his powers. The new constitution allows citizens to review the records of government agencies, but the citizens will need to be active in many ways to preserve and protect their role as a watchdog over their government. If the citizenry is passive or inactive, bureaucrats, politicians, and the military can easily run amok.

Leaving Thailand is often difficult for visitors. The charm and welcoming attitude of the people and culture are both enchanting and addictive. The beauty of the land only adds to the difficulty of ending an adventure in Thailand. Writer Ellen Peck traveled to Siam in March 1906. Her book *Travels in the Far East*, published in 1909, provides us with a closing thought on the future of Thailand: "With all the available information about the kingdom of Siam, one cannot but feel that it has a future full of possibilities." The sentiment written a century ago echoes loud and clear today, and there is little doubt that the future of Thailand is still more than filled with possibilities. Hopefully, it will also include the possibility of our return to the country through books or through travel.

Facts at a Glance

Physical Geography

Location Southeastern Asia, bordering the Andaman Sea and the Gulf of Thailand, southeast of Myanmar

Area Total: 198,115 square miles (513,115 square kilometers); land: 197,599 square miles (511,779 square kilometers); water: 861 square miles (2,230 square kilometers); slightly more than twice the size of Wyoming

Climate Tropical: rainy, warm, cloudy southwest monsoon (mid-May to September); dry, cool northeast monsoon (November to mid-March); southern isthmus always hot and humid

Terrain Central plain; Khorat Plateau in the east; mountains elsewhere

Elevation Extremes Lowest point is the Gulf of Thailand (sea level); highest point is Doi Inthanon, 8,451 feet (2,576 meters)

Land Use Arable land, 27.54%; permanent crops, 6.93%; other, 65.53% (2005)

Irrigated Land 19,251 square miles (49,860 square kilometers) (2003)

Natural Hazards Land subsidence in Bangkok area resulting from the depletion of the water table; droughts, tsunami

Natural Resources Tin, rubber, natural gas, tungsten, tantalum, timber, lead, fish, gypsum, lignite, fluorite, arable land

Environmental Issues Air pollution from vehicle emissions; water pollution from organic and factory wastes; deforestation; soil erosion; wildlife populations threatened by illegal hunting

People

Population 64,631,595 (July 2006 est.); males, 31,970,570 (2006 est.); females, 32,661,025 (2006 est.)

Population Density 326 people per square mile (126 per square kilometer)

Population Growth Rate 0.68% (2006 est.)

Net Migration Rate 0 migrant(s)/1,000 population (2006 est.)

Fertility Rate 1.64 children born/woman (2006 est.)

Life Expectancy at Birth Total population: 72.25 years; male, 69.95 years; female, 74.68 years (2006 est.)

Median Age 31.9 years; male, 31.1 years; female, 32.8 years (2006 est.)

Ethnic Groups Thai, 75%, Chinese, 14%, others, 11%

Religions Buddhist, 94.6%, Muslim, 4.6%, Christian, 0.7%

Languages Thai, English, ethnic and regional dialects

Literacy	(Age 15 and over can read and write) Total population: 92.6% (male, 94.9%; female, 90.5%) (2002 est.)

Economy

Currency	Baht
GDP Purchasing Power Parity (PPP)	$560.7 billion (2005 est.)
GDP Per Capita (PPP)	$8,300 (2005 est.)
Labor Force	35.36 million
Unemployment	1.4% (2005)
Labor Force by Occupation	Agriculture, 49%; services, 37%; industry, 14%
Agricultural Products	Rice, cassava (tapioca), rubber, corn, sugarcane, coconuts, soybeans
Industries	Tourism, textiles and garments, agricultural processing, beverages, tobacco, cement, light manufacturing such as jewelry and electric appliances, computers and parts, integrated circuits, furniture, plastics, automobiles and automotive parts, tungsten, tin
Exports	$105.8 billion (2005 est.)
Imports	$107 billion (2005 est.)
Leading Trade Partners	Exports: U.S., 16.1%; Japan, 14%; China, 7.4%; Singapore, 7.3%; Malaysia, 5.5%; Hong Kong, 5.1% Imports: Japan, 23.7%; China, 8.7%; U.S., 7.7%; Malaysia, 5.9%; Singapore, 4.4%; Taiwan, 4.1% (2004)
Export Commodities	Textiles and footwear, fishery products, rice, rubber, jewelry, automobiles, computers, and electrical appliances
Import Commodities	Capital goods, intermediate goods and raw materials, consumer goods, fuels
Transportation	Roadways: 35,670 miles (57,403 kilometers), of which 35,135 miles (56,542 kilometers) are paved (2003); Airports: 108–66 are paved runways (2006); Waterways: 2,486 miles (4,000 kilometers)

Government

Country Name	Conventional long form: Kingdom of Thailand; Conventional short form: Thailand; Local long form: Ratcha Anachak Thai; Local short form: Prathet Thai; Former: Siam

Capital City	Bangkok
Type of Government	Constitutional monarchy
Head of Government	Interim Prime Minister Surayud Chulanont (since October 1, 2006)
Independence	1238 (traditional founding date; never colonized)
Administrative Divisions	76 provinces

Communications

TV Stations	111 (2006)
Phones	(Line) 6,797,000 million; (cell) 27,379,000
Internet Users	8,420,000 (2005)

* Source: CIA-The World Factbook (2006)

3,000+ B.C.	Rice growing cultures exist in the Ban Chieng area.
566	Siddhartha Gautama (Buddha) born in India.
A.D. **650**	Thai Nanchao kingdom formed in Yunnan, China.
1238	Kingdom of Sukhothai established, start of Thai independence; Theravada Buddhism designated as the official religion of the Sukhothai Dynasty.
1253	Mongols, under Kublai Khan, conquer Nanchao.
1277	King Ramkhamhaeng Kamheng comes to power and later is referred to as Rama the Great.
1283	King Ramkhamhaeng Kamheng introduces Thai language.
1317	Rama the Great dies.
1350	Ayutthaya founded by U Thong, who becomes known as Rama the Brave.
1369	U Thong dies.
1383	Wat Phra That Doi Suthep Temple built near Chiang Mai.
1431	Ayutthaya forces conquer the Khmer city of Angkor.
1511	The first Portuguese arrive with missionaries and traders.
1558	Chiang Mai conquered by Burma.
1592	Rice treaty signed between Ayutthaya and the Dutch.
1657	King Narai comes to power.
1664	King Narai calls upon the French to counterbalance the more hostile presence of the Dutch.
1688	King Narai dies and Phra Phetracha seizes the throne and ends most Thai contact with Europeans (which lasts for nearly 150 years).
1693	Phra Phetracha dies.
1767	Ayutthaya's era as the capital ends.
1774	Chiang Mai freed from Burma by King Taksin.
1782	King Taksin is pushed out of power and General Chakkri takes over; General Chakkri changes name to King Rama I and establishes Bangkok as his capital on the Chao Phraya River.
1786	Sunthorn Phu, Thailand's poet laureate, is born.

1809	Rama I dies but starts the succession of kings of Siam that still exists today.
1826	Khun Ying Mo leads effort to repulse Laotian invasion and protect Khorat Burney; treaty signed between Thailand and British.
1833	Trade and commerce agreement signed between Thailand and the United States.
1850	Phuket elevated to town status.
1851	Rama III (Nang Klao) dies and Mongkut becomes Rama IV.
1868	Rama IV dies and Chulalongkorn becomes Rama V.
1893	Thai claims to Laos end.
1897	Railroad between Ayutthaya and Bangkok completed.
1907	Thai claims to Cambodia end.
1910	Rama V dies and Vajiravudh becomes Rama VI.
1917	Thailand joins the Allies and declares war on Germany.
1919	Thailand becomes a founding member of the League of Nations.
1925	Rama VI dies at the age of 44 and is followed by Prajadhipok (Rama VII).
1932	Constitutional monarchy begins with a coup.
1934	Thao Suranari Monument erected in Khorat to honor Khun Ying Mo.
1935	Prajadhipok (Rama VII) abdicates throne.
1938	Pibal Songgram becomes prime minister.
1939	Country name changes to Thailand from the Kingdom of Siam.
1942	Thailand declares war on the United States and Allies but Thai ambassador Seni Pramoj doesn't deliver the declaration to the U.S. government.
1944	Pibal Songgram forced out of government and a civilian government reinstated.
1945	Seni Pramoj becomes prime minister.

1946	Bhumibol Adulyadej becomes Rama IX upon the sudden death of Ananda Mahidol (Rama VIII).
1947	Pibal Songgram leads a military coup and assumes power.
1958	Pibal Songgram's government forced out in a military coup.
1962	U.S. military base operations for Vietnam begin at the Royal Thai Air Force base in Khorat.
1964	Pibal Songgram dies in exile in Japan.
1967	Thailand is a founding member of the Association of Southeast Asian Nations (ASEAN).
1975	United States ends use of Khorat military base for Vietnam operations.
1983	Pridi Phanomyang dies in France.
1984	First cases in Thailand of HIV/AIDS.
1992	Civilian revolt against military rule forces elections.
1997	Asian financial crisis begins; New Thai constitution implemented.
1999	Sky Train opens in Bangkok.
2001	Thaksin Shinawatra becomes prime minister.
2004	Devastating tsunami strikes Phuket and west seacoast of Thailand with thousands dead and injured.
2005	Thai Rak Thai Party (TRT) gains control of the National Assembly with election.
2006	New Bangkok International Airport opens; Prime Minister Thaksin indicted for fraud and tax evasion; Bhumibol Adulyadej (Rama IX) celebrates sixtieth year on throne; September military coup d'etat.

Bibliography

Agar, Charles. *Frommer's Thailand.* Hoboken, N.J.: Wiley Publishing, 2004.

Baker, Chris, and Pasuk Phongpaichit. *A History of Thailand.* Cambridge, U.K.: Cambridge University Press, 2005.

Cummings, Joe, Sandra Bao, Steven Martin, and China Williams. *Lonely Planet Thailand.* Victoria, Australia: Lonely Planet Publications, 2003.

Hoare, Timothy, and Lucien Ellington, ed. *Thailand: A Global Studies Handbook.* Santa Barbara, Calif.: ABC-CLIO, 2004.

Jones, Roger. *Culture Smart: Thailand: A Quick Guide to Customs and Etiquette.* Portland, Ore.: Graphic Arts Center Publishing Company, 2003.

Kislenko, Arne. *Culture and Customs of Thailand.* Westport, Conn.: Greenwood Press, 2004

Peck, Ellen M.H. *Travels in the Far East.* New York: Thomas Y. Crowell & Co., 1909.

Phillips, Douglas A. *Southeast Asia.* Philadelphia: Chelsea House Publishers, 2006.

——, and Steven C. Levi. *The Pacific Rim Region: Emerging Giant.* Hillside, N.J.: Enslow Publishers, 1988.

Weightman, Barbara A. *Dragons and Tigers: A Geography of South, East, and Southeast Asia, Updated Edition.* New York: John Wiley & Sons, 2004.

Wyatt, David K. *Thailand: A Short History.* New Haven, Conn.: Yale University Press, 2003.

Baxter, Craig, Yogendra K. Malik, Charles H. Kennedy, and Robert C. Oberst. *Government and Politics in South Asia.* Boulder, Colo.: Westview Press, 2001.

Gupta, Avijit. *The Physical Geography of Southeast Asia* (Oxford Regional Environments). Oxford, U.K.: Oxford University Press, 2005.

Heidhues, Mary Somer. *Southeast Asia: A Concise History.* London: Thames & Hudson, 2001.

Higham, Charles. *Early Cultures of Mainland Southeast Asia.* Chicago: Art Media Resources, 2003.

Leinbach, Thomas R., and Richard Ulack. *Southeast Asia: Diversity and Development.* New York: Prentice-Hall, 1999.

McCloud, Donald G. *Southeast Asia: Tradition and Modernity in the Contemporary World.* Boulder, Colo.: Westview Press, 1995.

Nesadurai, Helen Sharmini. *Globalization, Domestic Politics and Regionalism: The ASEAN Free Trade Area.* London: Routledge, 2003.

Osborne, Milton. *Southeast Asia: An Introductory History.* New South Wales, Australia: Allen & Unwin Pty., 2001.

Owen, Norman G., David Chandler, and William R. Roff. *The Emergence of Modern Southeast Asia: A New History.* Honolulu: University of Hawaii Press, 2004.

Parkes, Carl. *Southeast Asia (Moon Handbooks).* Emeryville, Calif.: Avelon Travel Publishing, 2001.

Phongpaichit, Pasuk, and Chris Baker. *Thailand Economy and Politics.* Oxford, U.K.: Oxford University Press, 2002.

Rawson, Philip S. *The Art of Southeast Asia: Cambodia Vietnam Thailand Laos Burma Java Bali (World of Art).* London: Thames & Hudson, 1990.

Rigg, Jonathon. *Southeast Asia: A Region in Transition: A Thematic Human Geography of the Asean Region.* New South Wales, Australia: Allen & Unwin Pty., 1991.

Sardesai, D.R. *Southeast Asia: Past & Present.* Boulder, Colo.: Westview Press, 2003.

Tarling, Nicholas. *The Cambridge History of Southeast Asia.* Cambridge, U.K.: Cambridge University Press, 1999.

———. *Nations and States in Southeast Asia.* Cambridge: Cambridge, U.K. University Press, 1998.

Warren, William, and Luca Invernizzi Tettoni. *Thailand: The Golden Kingdom*. North Clarendon, Vt.: Periplus Editions, 1999.

Web sites

CIA—The World Factbook
https://www.cia.gov/cia/publications/factbook/geos/th.html

Kingdom of Thailand
http://www.kingdom-of-thailand.com/

U.S Department of State—Background Note on Thailand
http://www.state.gov/r/pa/ei/bgn/2814.htm

Geography of Thailand
http://www.thailandguidebook.com/geography.html

Project Thailand
http://www.thaistudents.com/project/index.html

absolute monarchies, 50–51
agriculture
    deforestation and, 23
    economy and, 66, 67–68
    Khorat and, 82
    Phuket and, 85
    water pollution and, 22–23
AIDS, 40, 48–49, 69–70
air pollution, 22
airports, 71, 80, 81, 84–85
alcohol, Buddhism and, 42
alluvial plains, 17–19
alphabets, 26
al-Qaeda, 44, 88
Amnesty International, 63
Andaman Sea, 11, 20–21, 83–84
Angkor Wat, 82
Ankor, 28
Anna and the King, 24
aquaculture, 23
architecture, 40
area of Thailand, 11, 12
arts, 40
Asia Europe Meeting (ASEM), 75
Asian financial crisis, 37, 66
Asia-Pacific Economic Corporation
    (APEC), 75
Association of Southeast Asian
    Nations (ASEAN), 36, 63–64, 65,
    74–75, 87–88
avian influenza, 68, 88, 89
Ayutthaya, 18, 22, 26–29, 69

Baht, 37, 66
Ban Chieng civilization, 25
Bang Nieng Beach, 21
Bangkok
    as capital, 9, 18, 31
    courts in, 60
    overview of, 77–80
    pollution and, 22
    transportation infrastructure in,
        72–73
Bangkok International Airport, 71, 80

Bangkok Post, 74
Bangkok Tropical Cyclone Warning
    Center, 21
Bay of Bengal, 19
bells, temples and, 81
Bhumibol Adulyadej (King), 13,
    36–37, 43, 54–56, 87
Bilauktaung Range, 17
biodiversity, deforestation and, 23
bird flu, 68, 88, 89
Britain, history of Thailand and, 28,
    31
Buddhism
    class structure and, 29–30
    culture and, 39, 41–43
    neutrality and, 24
    overview of, 41–43
    Rama IV and, 31–32
    status of women and, 49
    Theravada, 26, 42
    touching of heads and, 9
buffer state, Thailand as, 32–33
Burma
    Ayutthaya era and, 30
    as bordering country, 10–11, 12, 29
    Chiang Mai and, 81
    natural gas and, 71
Burney Treaty, 31
bus system, 71–72

Cambodia, 11, 12, 29, 30, 82
canals, 19, 78
cassava, 68
censorship, 74
Chao Phraya Chakkri, 30–31, 78
Chao Phraya River, 17–18, 26, 78, 81
Chart Thai Party (TNP), 59
Chavalit Yongchaiyudh, 66
Chevron Texaco, 71
Chi River, 17
Chiang Mai, 28, 80–81
Chiang Mai International Airport, 71,
    81
Chiang Rai, 71

Index

China, 25–28, 30
cholera, 26
Christianity, 43, 44
Chulalongkorn, 31–33, 87
citizens, government and, 61–63
City of Angels. *See* Bangkok
civilian rule, military rule vs., 33–38, 87
class structure of historical Thailand,
    29–30
classical dance, 46, 47
climate and weather, 15, 19–20
colonialism, lack of, 11, 24
communication, economy and, 73–74
constitution, 51–54, 88–89
constitutional monarchies, 51
Constitutional Tribunal, 60
Convention on Biological Diversity
    (CBD), 23
copper, Khorat and, 82
corruption, 37, 88–89, 91
Council of Ministers, 57
coups, 11–12, 33, 50–51, 60, 90–91
courts, overview of, 60
Courts of First Instance, 60
crickets, as food, 48
crops, 15, 18–19
culture
    Buddhism and, 41–43
    characteristics of people and, 40–41
    food and, 46–48
    issues facing people and culture
        and, 48–49
    language and literature and, 44–45
    music and dance and, 45–46
    overview of, 39–40
    religions other than Buddhism and,
        43–44
currency, 37, 66
cyclones, 21

Daily News, 74
dances, 40, 45–46, 47
Dawna Range, 17
deforestation, 23
democracy, constitutions and, 51–53
Democratic Party (DP), 59

development, deforestation and, 23
dictatorships, defined, 52
diplomacy, history of Thailand and,
    28–29
discrimination, Muslims and, 44
District Courts, 60
Doi Inthanon National Park, 15
Doi Suthep, 81
Dong Muang Royal Thai Air Force
    Base, 80
drought, 21–22
drugs, 15–16, 42, 79, 81, 88
dry monsoon, 20

earthquakes, 20–21
economy
    agriculture and, 66, 67–68, 85
    Asian financial crisis and, 37, 66
    Association of Southeast Asian
        Nations (ASEAN) and, 36
    Bangkok and, 79–80
    communication and, 73–74
    foreign trade and, 74–75
    future of Thailand and, 87
    manufacturing and, 68–69
    natural resources and, 70–71
    northern region and, 15–16
    overview of, 40–41, 65–66, 75–76
    Phuket and, 85
    pollution and, 22
    tourism and, 69–70, 85, 87–88
    transportation infrastructure and,
        71–73
education, 32, 33, 40, 57
electricity, 71
environment
    future of Thailand and, 88–89
    hazards of, 20–22
    human impact on, 15, 22–23, 79
    natural resources and, 70–71
    overview of, 14–15
erosion, 23
executive branch of government, 57

fauna, 15, 17
feet, Buddhism and, 9

flooding, 15, 20, 21
flora, 17
folk dance, 46, 47
food, culture and, 46–48
foreign policy, 63–64
foreign trade. See trade
forests, 23
France, 28–29
freedom of speech, 52
future of Thailand, 86–91

Gautama, Siddhartha, 41–42
General Provisions, 52
geography, overview of, 9–11
Golden Temple, 22, 69
Golden Triangle, 15, 81, 88
government
    constitution and, 51–54
    courts and, 60
    executive branch of, 57
    foreign policy and, 63–64
    legislative branch of, 58–60
    overview of, 11–12, 50–51
    provincial and local, 60–61
    Rama V and, 32, 33
    role of citizens in, 61–63
    role of kings in, 54–57
governors, 60
Grand Palace, 42, 43, 80
gross domestic product (GDP), 40
    pollution and, 22
Gulf of Thailand, 11, 19

Hat Yai International Airport, 71
heads, touching of, 9
heroin, 17
history of Thailand
    Ayutthaya and, 26–28
    Chakkri Dynasty and, 30–33
    constitutional era and, 33–38
    early, 25–26
    European trade and, 28–30
HIV-AIDS, 40, 48–49, 69–70
holidays, Buddhism and, 42–43
House of Representatives, 57, 58
Hua Hin, 33

human rights, 61–63
humidity, 19–20
hurricanes, 21

India, 41, 45
inflation, Vietnam War and, 36
insects, as food, 48
International Monetary Fund, 75
international policy, 63–64
internet, 73
Islam, 43–44
islands, 19. See also Phuket

Japan, 11, 28–29, 34–35
Jemaah Islamiyah, 44, 88

Karen Padaung tribe, 9, 10
Karen tribes, 9
Khao Lak, 20–21
Khao Sod, 74
Khmer alphabet, 26
Khorat, overview of, 82
Khorat Plateau, 10, 16, 17
khruang sai music, 46
Khun Ying Mo, 82, 83
The King and I, 24
Kingdom of Siam, 8
kings. See also specific kings
    Chakkri lineage and, 31
    role of, 11–13, 30, 54–57
Klong Toey Port, 80
Kom Chad Leuk, 74
Koran, 43
Kra Isthmus, 16, 19
Kublai Khan, 25, 26

Laem Chabang, 73, 80
landscapes, 15–19
landslides, 21
languages, 25, 39, 44–45
Laos, 11, 12, 29, 30, 82
latex, 67
League of Nations, 33
legal code, Ramathibodi I and, 27
legislative branch of government,
    58–60

Index

life expectancy, 41
lignite coal, 70
literacy, 40
literature, culture and, 44–45
livestock, Khorat and, 82
local governments, 60–61
long-neck women, 9, 10
Lopburi River, 26
luck, 9
luk thung music, 46
lychee, 15

Malay Peninsula, 16, 19, 28
Malaysia, 11, 12, 19, 44
Manchuria, 34–35
manufacturing, economy and, 68–69
media, restrictions on, 63
Mekong River, 10, 17
Menom, 19
military rule, civilian rule vs., 33–38,
    87
mineral wealth, 70, 82
ministries, 57
Ministry of the Interior, 61
monarchies, 50–51
Mongkut, 31–32
monks, class structure and, 29–30
monsoons, 20
mountains, 19, 81
Mun River, 17
music, culture and, 45–46
Muslim faith, 43–44
Muslim separatists, 37, 62, 88
Myanmar. See Burma

Nakhon Ratchasima, overview of, 82
Nakon Sawan, 15
Nan River, 15
Nanchao kingdom, 25
Nang Klao, 31
Narai (King), 28–29
The Nation, 74
National Assembly, 56–57, 58–60
natural gas, 70, 71
natural resources, economy and,
    70–71

necks, Karen Padaung tribe and, 9, 10
Netherlands, history of Thailand and,
    28–29
New Bangkok International Airport,
    71, 80
newspapers, 74
Nirats, 45
nobility, class structure and, 29–30

oil industry, 70–71, 75
opium, 15–17, 81
Ordinary Sessions, 58

parks, 15, 82
Parliament building, 78
Pasak River, 26
Pattaya, 69
Pearl of the Andaman, 83
Peck, Ellen, 91
People's Party, 33–34
Petroleum Authority of Thailand, 71
Phang Nga Province, 84
Phetchabun Mountains, 17
Phnom Dangrek Range, 17
phone system, 73
Phra Aphai Mani, 45
Phra Mangala Bophit, 42
Phra Phetracha, 29
Phraya Taksin, 30
Phuket, 20–21, 69, 82–85
Phuket International Airport, 71,
    84–85
Pibul Songgram, 33–35
Ping River, 15, 81
piphat music, 45
Plam Piang Din Village, 9
poets, 45
politics, overview of, 11–12
pollution, 22–23, 79
poppy fields, 15
population
    of Bangkok, 78
    of Chiang Mai, 80
    estimation of, 11, 12
    growth and, 23, 41
ports, 73, 80

Portuguese, trade and, 28
postal system, 73
pottery, history of Thailand and, 25
poultry, 68
poverty, Muslims and, 44
Prachuap, 73
Prajadhipok, 33–34, 87
Pramoj, Seni, 35
prayer, Islam and, 44
Pridi Phanomyong, 33–35
prime minister, role of, 57
Privy Council, 56
prostitution, 40, 48–49, 69
provincial governments, 60–61
Provincial Juvenile Courts, 60
PTT, 70–71
Pumpuang Duangjan, 46

radio, 73
rain forests, 19, 23, 70
rainfall, 19–20
Rama I, 30–31, 78
Rama III, 31
Rama IV, 31–32
Rama V, 31–33, 87
Rama VI, 33
Rama VII, 33–34, 87
Rama IX, 13, 36–37, 43, 54–56, 87
Rama the Great, 26
Ramakien, 45
Ramathibodi I, 26–27
Ramayana, 45
Ramkhamhaeng Kamheng, 26
religion, 43–44, 52, 56. See also
    Buddhism
rice, 18–19, 25, 28, 48, 67, 82
rivers, 15, 17, 23, 26, 70
Royal Thai Army, 73, 82, 90, 91
rubber, 67

Sandika, 60
Sapha Phuthaen Ratsadon, 57, 58
Sarnath, 41
savanna region, 19–20
Senate, 58
Seni Pramoj, 35

sexually transmitted diseases, 40,
    48–49, 69–70
Shin Corporation, 73
shipping, 73, 80
shrimp, aquaculture and, 23
Si Racha, 73
Siam, 8
Sino-Tibetan language family, 45
Sirikit (Queen), 55
Sky Train, 72, 79
slavery, Rama V and, 32, 33
slaves, class structure and, 29–30
Social Commission for Asia and the
    Pacific (ESCAP), 75
Songkhla, 60, 80
spices, 46–48
stamps, 73
Strait of Malaca, 19, 28
Suchinda Kraprayoon, 56
Sukhothai Dynasty, 25–26, 27
Sunthorn Phu, 45
Supreme Court, 60
Surayud Chulanont, 90, 91
Suvarnabhumi, 71, 80

Tang Dynasty, history of Thailand
    and, 25
tax evasion, 37
teak, 15
telegraph, Rama V and, 33
television, 73
Temple of the Emerald Buddha, 42, 78
temples, 27, 81. See also specific tem-
    ples
Texaco, 71
textiles, 25, 68–69
Thai Rak Thai Party (TRT), 58–59
Thai Rath, 74
Thaksin Shinawatra, 37, 59–60, 90, 91
Thao Suranari, 82, 83
Theravada Buddhism, 26, 42
Thonburi, 30
Tibet, 25
timber, 70
tin, 70
TNP, 59

Index

tobacco, Khorat and, 82
tourism, 19, 69–70, 80, 85, 87–88
trade. *See also* Association of
    Southeast Asian Nations
    (ASEAN)
  economy and, 74–75
  history of Thailand and, 28, 29
  Phuket and, 84
  treaties and, 31
traffic, Bangkok and, 78–79
trains, 33, 71–72
transparency, financial, 66
transportation infrastructure, 71–73,
    78–79, 81
Travels in the Far East, 91
Treaty of Amity and Commerce, 31
tsunamis, 20–22, 37, 85, 87–88
tuk-tuks, 9, 72–73
tungsten, 70

U Thong, 26–27
United Nations Environment
    Programme (UNEP), 22
United States, 31, 36, 82
United States-Asia Environmental
    Partnership (US-AEP), 22
Unocal, 71

Vajiravudh, 33
Vietnam War, 36, 49, 82

violence, 62
voting, 58

wai, 8, 9
Wang River, 15
war, declarations of, 56
warning systems for environmental
    hazards, 21–22
wat, defined, 70
Wat Chai Watthanaram temple, 27
Wat Chiang Man, 81
Wat Phra Kaew, 43
Wat Phra That Doi Suthep Temple, 81
water pollution, 22–23, 79
weather and climate, 15, 19–20
wildlife, 15, 23
women, prostitution and, 40, 48–49,
    69
World Heritage Sites, 27, 69
World Intellectual Property
    Organization (WIPO), 75
World Trade Organization (WTO), 75
World War I, 11, 33
World War II, 11, 34–35
Wuthisapha, 58

Yala Islamic College, 62
Yom River, 15
Yuan Dynasty, 25

page:

About the Contributors

Author DOUGLAS A. PHILLIPS is a lifetime educator, writer, and consultant who has worked and traveled in more than 100 countries on six continents. During his career, he has worked as a middle school teacher, as a curriculum developer, as an author, and as a trainer of educators in many countries around the world. He has served as the president of the National Council for Geographic Education and has received the Outstanding Service Award from the National Council for the Social Studies, along with numerous other awards. He, his wife, Marlene, and their three children, Chris, Angela, and Daniel, have lived in South Dakota and Alaska. His daughter is now in Texas, while he, his wife, and his two sons now reside in Arizona, where he writes and serves as an educational consultant for the Center for Civic Education. He has traveled in Thailand and understands the people and incredible culture of the country.

Series editor CHARLES F. GRITZNER is distinguished professor of geography at South Dakota State University in Brookings. He is now in his fifth decade of college teaching, research, and writing. In addition to teaching, he enjoys writing, working with teachers, and sharing his love of geography with readers. As series editor for Chelsea House's MODERN WORLD NATIONS (and other) series, he has had a wonderful opportunity to combine these interests. Gritzner has served as both president and executive director of the National Council for Geographic Education. He also has received many national honors, including the George J. Miller Award for Distinguished Service to Geographic Education from the NCGE and both the Distinguished Teaching Achievement Award and the Gilbert Grosvenor Honors in Geographic Education from the Association of American Geographers.